Mindful Smart Cities

Mindful Smart Cities

Rethinking Smart Cities
with Mindfulness Engineering™

Shima Beigi, PhD.
Founder of Mindfulness Engineering™
Resilience Scientist and Smart City Expert

Cover design: Jeroen Bergen
Typesetting: theSWitch

© 2020 VUBPRESS
VUBPRESS is an imprint of ASP nv
(Academic and Scientific Publishers)
Keizerslaan 34
1000 Brussels
Tel. +32 (0)2 289 26 56
Fax +32 (0)2 289 26 59
Email: info@aspeditions.be
www.vubpress.be

ISBN 978 90 5718 083 5
NUR 740
Legal deposit D/2020/11.161/023

This Manifesto is dedicated to the past, present and future generations.
In the memory of those that have lost their lives in the fight for freedom,
solidarity and liberty.
In honour of my mentors, Professor Colin A. Taylor, Professor Francis
Heylighen, Professor Wolfgang Hofkirchner, and Dr. Harry Halpin.
In honour of my alma maters, University of Oxford, and University
of Bristol.
In honour of my spiritual teachers, Thomas Huble, Baba Ram Dass,
and Rabbi Manis Friedman.
In honour of the incredible people of India, Indonesia, and Iran.
In honour of the magic of European Cities and Citizens.
In honour of the beauty of our Earth.
In honour of my family.
I write to empower the next generation of scientists, technologists,
mathematicians, engineers and those that seek truth in today's
noisy world.
Together we can create a future that is about love, compassion, inclusion,
and freedom of expression.
Technology Connects. But, it is the human connection that
brings consciousness.

I was ready to tell
the story of my life
but the ripples of tears
and the agony of my heart
wouldn't let me
I began to stutter
saying a word here and there
and all along I felt
as tender as a crystal
ready to be shattered
in this stormy sea
we call life
All the big ships
come apart
board by board
How can I survive
riding a lonely little boat
with no oars and no arms
My boat did finally break
upon the waves
and I broke free
as I tied myself
to a single board
Though the panic is gone
i am now offended
Why should I be so helpless
rising with one wave
and falling with the next
I don't know

if I am
nonexistence
while I exist
but I know
if I am
nonexistence
while I exist
But i know for sure
when I am
I am not
but
when I am not
then I am
Now how can I be
a sceptic
about the resurrection
and coming life again
since in this world
I have many times
like my own imagination
died and been born again
That is why
after a long organising life
as a hunter
I finally let go and got
hunted down and became free.

Rumi
Fountain of Fire

CONTENT

List of abbreviations   8

Foreword   9

The Birth of the Mindful Smart City Manifesto   15

Chapter 1 Rethinking Smart Cities with Mindfulness
           Engineering™   21

Chapter 2 Shifting the Techno-Centric View of Smartness   35

Chapter 3 Why Re-Think Smart Cities with Mindfulness
           Engineering?   41

Chapter 4 It's About Smartfulness®   57

Chapter 5 The Mindful Smart City   71

Chapter 6 The Right to Technology   87

Chapter 7 Preserving the Right to Becoming in the
           Age of GUD   95

What is Next?   103

References   105

LIST OF ABBREVIATIONS

Information Communication Technology (ICT)
Artificial Intelligence (AI)
Internet of Things (IoT)
Internet of People (IoP)
Globalisation, Digitalisation and Urbanisation (GUD)
New Generation of Internet (NGI)
Command and Control (CC)
Resilient Agent (RA)
Resilient Living Spaces (RLS)
Resilient Interfaces (RI)

FOREWORD

The moment of reckoning for smart cities is fast approaching, and Shima Beigi's *Mindful Smart Cities* Manifesto points us to a way out. Smart cities were once envisaged as a future where the estrangement of social space and corporate technology could be reconciled, as noted by Beigi in the pioneering work of Béatrice van Bastelaer's *Digital Cities and Transferability of Results*. The vast network of sensors and data collection of the smart city would promise less pollution, smoother traffic, and an improved quality of life. Years ago, when I was reviewing the results of attempts to create new sensor-driven 'smart' public transportation in Val-de-Marne outside Paris, it became clear there was a problem: The locals were destroying the shiny new 'smart' bus stops.

Were they right to do so? Smart cities are increasingly considered as the latest frontier of a totalitarian panopticon, and protests against smart city projects like Quayside in Toronto have just declared victories. While the general public knows about the digital violations of their private lives via tracking by browsers and mobile phones, smart cities are applying these measures of surveillance to our public lives. Privacy has as its root the defence of private individual life from the paparazzi of the public sphere, but the same techniques of surveillance are now eroding that public sphere. Perhaps 'privacy' is not even the right word, etymologically speaking: Constant monitoring, facial recognition via artificial intelligence, and predictive policing carry the danger that smart cities will be the final step of the dissolution of the public agora inside of a vast and opaque surveillance machine.

Shima Beigi is a remarkable interdisciplinary scholar of resilience, a field in which she has pioneered the application of a whole different paradigm of possibilities to smart cities: What if smart cities could be founded on a set of values that made us more mindful of our world, rather than optimise for efficiency? Her concept of *mindful smart cities* is based on a proposition that I strongly agree with: "Human beings are not programmable. This means that there are parts of human existence namely human spirit, spontaneity, creativity, curiosity, empathy, and love that cannot be programmed and manipulated with, or by, AI." Engineers often assume that by merely connecting things via digital networks they can restore a fragmented city that is hard to understand and even live in. In all these fantasies of engineers, technology ends up transcending humanity into a digital sublime, where all that is human evaporates. In contrast, mindfulness reconnects us with each other using human emotions. What is new and controversial about Beigi's approach is that she states that the smart city can extend and deepen these emotions via technology, leading to a reconciliation between our embodied consciousness and the world in which we are embedded.

As pointed out by Brian Cantwell Smith, the technological explosion of Western civilisation began with a stripping away of spirit from mechanism, where the only kind of scientific intelligence allowed was a European masculine rationality that simply abolished the questions of the spirit that had occupied the Christian tradition since the fall of Rome. However, it is precisely these questions, of how a certain arrangement of atoms can be imbued with meaning and significance, that are left unanswered by science. Attempts to create a more holistic understanding of the world, such as cybernetics, have equally been erected on a fairly limited European scientific tradition. Yet these questions have been under intense consideration by Eastern philosophies that put ethical and social considerations at the forefront. No one is better positioned to synthesise the Eastern and Western traditions than Shima Beigi. Born in Iran, she is trained in science at universities such as Oxford and Vrije Universiteit Brussel, and she is a life-long student of Eastern philosophies of consciousness and spirituality. I consider myself exceedingly lucky to have encountered her and shared many extensive discussions on her research, which this book will help bring to the world. Putting together studies of complex adaptive systems with urban sustainability – but also the work of Henri Lefebvre and David Harvey on "the right to the city" – she points us to a new role for smart cities.

Her book's daring proposition is that the advent of smart cities can allow us to become mindful and more resilient rather than objects of surveillance and control. She outlines how mindfulness can be accomplished via the right to democratic participation in the creation of a new social space that, rather than destroying the ancient social traditions of many cities, deepens the rich connections that cities give us by extending them through digital technology. What makes Shima Beigi's thesis so remarkable is that it responds to the all-apparent need for spiritual answers with a new trajectory of technological development based on a mentality that honours the best of both the East and West, a collective intelligence rather than an artificial intelligence.

Given the scope of the crisis provoked by COVID-19, resiliency is needed more than ever. The re-marking of the smart city envisioned by Beigi is of pronounced importance in the midst of this pandemic, now that people are forced to stay inside their homes and their social connection to the outside world mainly takes place via an array of screens and devices. The traditional city social life that has already been atrophied by capitalism seemingly disappears entirely in this situation, and is replaced by surveillance in the name of public health. Continuous surveillance could easily become normalised via smart cities, where sociality and travel restrictions are enforced via sensors and our lives cut off from each other. After all, the 'smart' in smart city only recently started being used to describe machines that seem intelligent, such as the 'smart bomb'. The etymological origin of the term 'smart' in the medieval era refers to a sharp and painful cutting. We will have to choose whether we return to a smart city that promotes our humanity or one that cuts us away from each other. Thanks to the perspective given by Shima Beigi in this book, I am quietly confident that we can find a new kind of all-too-human connection in the era of the smart city.

Dr. Harry Halpin
Research Scientist
Inria
Paris, France

THE BIRTH OF THE MINDFUL SMART CITY MANIFESTO

When I think of a Manifesto, the most iconic pieces such as the Bible or the Ten Commandments, come to mind. These are iconic because they stemmed from divine revelations and led to clear trajectories for humanity. We can also think of the Humanist Manifesto, or the Declaration of Independence, or maybe the recent Leap Manifesto. All these works have one shared common denominator: the orientation of the human condition in a particular time in history. This Manifesto is rooted in the same origin. *Mindful Smart Cities: Rethinking Smart Cities with Mindfulness Engineering* is not written for the elites. Because we are striving through a critical time of human transition, which is signalling a gigantic shift in the meaning of governance, social status, labour, the nature of human relationships and business affairs, the future of scientific research, and the fate of ecological systems. Cities are about all of these things, and so is this Manifesto. This is a Manifesto for *real* people; men, women and children of all backgrounds, colours, all classes of society, regardless of their nationality. This is a Manifesto for those real soulful people who want to live in human-centric cities. These are the people that desire their cities to be sustainable, inclusive and welcoming. These are the people that want to call their cities their home and are not afraid to fall in love with the complex nature of urban systems. My position in writing this manifesto is more than that of simply being the founder of Mindfulness Engineering. I have lived in various cities and travelled to many regions around the world over the past twelve years. Fuelled by my scientific point of view and studies in the UK and Belgium, my vision combines the real struggles of adjusting to new cultures and urban layouts, my observations of the link between human nature and the impact of technology in shaping collective behaviour, and years of discussions with young scientists, artists, people and entrepreneurs who live their lives in cities. The current narrative of smart cities as cities that are intricately shaped by the invisible hand of technology is highly techno-centric. This should change. My aim is therefore to promote a CONSCIOUS, HUMAN-centric approach to the integration of digital platforms into the social, emotional, spiritual and cultural fabric of cities across the following chapters.

The Ten Commandments (10c) of the Mindful Smart City Manifesto

C1. Technology mechanically connects digital spaces. But, it's the HUMAN EMOTIONS that bring consciousness, awareness and intentionality into digital platforms. Therefore, we must focus on the Internet of People (IoP) instead of the Internet of Things (IoT). Smartness is not about how we connect objects through the fluid platform of the internet. Smartness is about our ability to use technology as a resource, as a potential for bringing forth the highest form of intelligence, i.e. self-actualisation and sense of agency.

C2. Human beings are not programmable. This means that *there are parts of human existence namely human spirit, spontaneity, creativity, curiosity, empathy, and love that cannot be programmed and manipulated with, or by, AI.*

C3. Mindfulness Engineering™ provides an alternative approach with the aim of rethinking the collective practice of knitting AI with human intelligence within the political and shared space of urban systems. In this view, Mindful Smart Cities are <u>not</u> about all data. They are about mindset, consciousness, intention, and vision fused with ICT.

C4. The Mindful Smart City Manifesto is about taking a systemic approach to Smart Cities, viewing cities as a mixture of a diverse range of complex adaptive systems, namely socio-ecological, socio-technical and psycho-social systems.

C5. Mindful Smart Cities are resilient and sustainable. Social systems and urban systems are not fixed points in space and time. A social system is a result of aggregation and self-organisation of human endeavours, and it clusters within hub-like entities, such as cities. Cities have a continuous demand for energy and resources from the surrounding environments and systems, in a similar way to biological organisms. With this dependency on the external elements, cities develop characteristics such as resilience, sustainability, liveability and smartness. These characteristics emerge from spontaneous dynamics between local interactions and sub-processes that run through and across them, as well as from the continuous and mutual adaptation of society, ecosystems, technical systems, technology, and other systems, to a changing environment.

C6. Mindful Smart Cities are interfaces. The majority of existing Smart City definitions adopt a utilitarian view with regard to ICT. Unlike the contemporary label of Smart Cities which has, to date, focused on ICT platforms, Mindfulness Engineering™ considers Smart Cities as interfaces; interfaces for understanding the intricate interdependence and interconnection of diverse potentialities. This means that the interface between technology and previous urban structures opens a completely new dimension for imagining cohesive living places.

C7. Mindfulness Engineering views Mindful Smart Cities as spaces of possibility with these goals: sustaining resilience of social-ecological-technical systems, customising innovative growth and evolution trends, and harnessing the cognitive capacities of resilient agents for the management of resilience.

C8. The Epigenetics of a Mindful Smart City are about connected people creating a field of energy filled with hope, love, empathy and happiness. Our thinking impacts not only our actions but also our biology. The intricate connection between behaviour and biology is explored with epigenetics. Mindfulness Engineering™ considers a similar relationship between socio-technical design and human behaviour.

C9. Mindfulness Engineering is focused toward the creation of WE SPACES. This dynamic ever-changing GUD landscape of the 21st century calls upon us to develop a roadmap by which to navigate between Known Knowns, Known Unknowns, Unknown Unknowns, and Unknown Knowns. The solution to this transition is working together as a global community in WE SPACES. For this level of collaboration to emerge, nevertheless, we must undergo not only a deep mental model transformation, but also a deep scientific revolution. We can solve the grand challenges of our time only by connecting ideas from different disciplines. And this means undergoing a fundamental transformation of ourselves (mentally, physically and spiritually).

C10. By extending the key features of mindfulness to the technological space – aka 'promoting inner calmness' – the notion of smart can be translated to Smartfulness. I define Smartfulness as being aware of connection to a higher consciousness, holding space for others, creating a gender-balanced notion of the smart city.

CHAPTER 1

RETHINKING SMART CITIES WITH MINDFULNESS ENGINEERING™

The core objective of this manifesto is about shifting the Smart City literature from a technological deterministic framework to a socio-technological over-deterministic one, where the core values of human communities are seen as powerful causative forces capable of redirecting the flow of novel technological mediums and their implementation. To enable this shift, and to mark a new developmental trajectory in the future of technology, I apply the framework of Mindfulness Engineering™ and the newly proposed initiative of the New Generation of Internet (NGI). The NGI endeavours to move toward a more human-centric internet that values openness, cooperation across borders, decentralisation, inclusiveness and giving control back to the users in order to increase trust in the internet. As more sensors, objects and AI programming integrate with our shared digital urban environment, translating fundamental concepts of urban sustainability such as urban inclusion, sense of place and social cohesion becomes increasingly complex. As shown below, the technological journey of MolenGeek has demonstrated that, due to the highly fragmented structure of Brussels, the traditional methods of Smart Cities, those that adopt ICT-centric visions, do not yield sustainable collective outcomes. This brings us back to the ethos of Mindfulness Engineering™; to become mindful of what serves communities and to understand that the cerebral monopoly of smartness does not appreciate the embedded bits and pieces of intelligence such as emotions, cultural reservoirs, and the landscape of feelings. These qualities represent different regions of the City of Brussels (i.e., Adam Greenfield's emphasis on the balance between leading cities versus controlling cities, and the harmony between mechanical cybernetic urban design versus creative and connected urban design). This is also an observation I made while living and working in Belgium. A rather large transitory population of expats, as well as the European Commission, in my philosophy, acts as an invisible hand, somewhat similar to Adam Smith's Invisible Hand, in creating socially temporal islands.

So what is a Smart City all about? First and foremost, a Smart City is thinking about finding ways to create Smart Agents by investing in people and their abilities to interact with not only digitalisation but also with the challenges of the 21st century. The second facet of Mindfulness Engineering™ is designing

Smart Living Spaces (i.e., incorporating appealing and inviting settings, with the aim of fostering Smartfulness). The third element of Mindfulness Engineering™ is creating Smart interfaces (i.e. building bridges between the formal and informal systems, changing paradigms).

In short, when we think about designing a Smart City, we must aim for thinking in terms of a system of interacting parts. Hence, we need to design for Smart Agents, Smart Living Spaces and Smart Interfaces at the same time. With this vision, this Manifesto aims to integrate the embedded bits of intelligence(s) such as emotions, skills, knowledge and ideas through bottom-up strategies, such as moving from the Internet of Things (IoT) towards the Internet of People (IoP).

Reading about Smart Cities, one cannot immediately realise the extent to which critical components such as experience, feelings, emotions and real human relationships are missing. What makes a city 'Smart' is not necessarily its technological competency, but rather the degree and quality of human connections and social cohesion that individuals feel. This is referring to commandment 3 and 1. I introduce the Internet of People (IoP) in parallel to the Internet of Things (IoT). With IoT we connect things. However, connecting things is mainly focused on the utilitarian use of ICT platforms. With the practice of Mindfulness Engineering™, the main aim of the design protocol is to make people, places and interfaces smart. Here, smart is defined based on the following principle: "There is a part of human existence that cannot be programmed and manipulated with and by AI". At best we can aim for *Satori*, or Enlightenment, through what Shanaham (2012) terms "AI plus", whereby humanity can overcome the problem of duality, i.e. separation between object and experience. This is indeed possible if we adopt a new mindset as to the design of future ICT platforms. And this is the primary aim of this Manifesto: a future that celebrates racial diversity, a future whereby, regardless of your religion or political views or point of origin, you are welcomed in co-creating a better future for everyone. This is what I call a Smart Mindful City, a Smart Soul, a Smart Living Being.

The Big Question: Where Does the Notion of Smart City Come From?

Smart cities first appeared in the literature during the 1990s. Béatrice van Bastelaer (1998) in *Digital Cities and Transferability of Results* put forward an argument on the seemingly increasing gap between the so-called traditional public and private sectors, increasing distance between people and the government, and the radical shift in the degree of globalisation and changes in the classic tendencies of the public sector in general. With this degree of complexity, van Bastelaer proposed the concept of digital cities as "laboratories of integration of multimedia technology within the public space".

The concept of Digital Cities was originally created as a 'business as usual' solution to facilitate communication between ever-disengaged communities and ever-frustrated governments within European cities. In other words, digital cities were originally seen as an alternative spatial dimension, termed an 'online community', for revitalising the broken and disrupted connection between people and governments. In short, the rationale behind the digital city makes the assumption that the problem of communication between people and government is a logical problem. As a result, it can be solved by introducing mechanical and managerial solutions. Since the appearance of digital cities, the feeling of loss of community, sense of belonging, membership and being a part of something bigger than oneself has become less and less appreciated, with the literature adopting a 'business as usual' approach, and filling itself with a broad range of mechanical formulations on how urban systems can become smart (i.e., digital). Two decades after the original conceptualisation, the literature of smart cities is yet to arrive at a universal framework, ideology, and definition of a Smart City.

Anthopoulos and Fitsilis (2013) argue that the conceptualisation of smart cities with regard to definitions and perspectives is still very confusing. Smart cities have already attracted the attention of scientific communities, political parties and industries. However, without a common platform, perspective or vision, these disciplines champion separated and isolated versions of the Smart City. Other scholars and practitioners have indeed widely expressed their concerns over this broad and disintegrated framework of smart cities, and have endeavoured to advocate for a foundation upon which future cities and digital ICT platforms should merge. For example, with the integration of ICT platforms with urban systems concepts such as sustainable development, social cohesion, place-making and sense of place, citizens and their rights to the city, resilience and adaptation to future shocks must be an integral – if not a core – aspect of smartification of societies and urban systems henceforth. Smartification of cities implies integration of artificial intelligence (AI) by means of sensors within cities' infrastructure systems for the purpose of virtually recreating and mimicking a portion of fundamental human cognitive capabilities such as learning and rational decision-making. As we rapidly move toward this format of smartification, Rodrigues argues that although technology facilitates interconnection of social and technical systems, issues such as governmentality, political dimensioning of data generation and data sharing must be at the forefront of the process of smartificiation. Therefore, it is necessary to take into account the underlying rationale upon which the conceptualisation of smart cities takes place, as well as the trade-offs that jeopardise the possibility of achieving a situation of spatial justice in urban systems (Rodrigues, 2016). I present the framework of Mindfulness Engineering™ as an alternative approach with the aim of rethinking the collective practice of knitting AI with human intelligence within the shared political, social, cultural, psychological, environmental and spiritual space of urban systems.

From Digital Cities to Digital Societies

The concept of Smart Cities emerged during the late 1990s under the notion of 'digital cities'. A digital city was set to be a solution to the ever-changing relationship and dynamics between people and governments, and between the private and public sectors. In the original vision of digital cities, the digital dimension would reconcile the weakened connection between public and the state, and would enable an indirect communication under the notion of 'online communities' (van Bastelaer, 1998).

Following its introduction, the concept of the digital city started to expand in a myriad of ways (Ishida and Isbister, 2000). The concept of Tele-Cities developed by Fathy (1991), for instance, leads digital cities into a different dimension. Fathy noticed that combination of technology with cities illustrated that the force of technology is not neutral. What Fathy describes as a non-neutrality of technology can be further investigated in Kevin Kelly's work on technology (2010). Technology is not neutral, it requires some form of input, just like biological organisms. Kelly uses the metaphor *technium*; "A global, massively interconnected system of technology vibrating around us", and advocates for the positive potentials of technology. Technology creates choice, and if we learn how to operate in this tech-induced choice landscape, we can become what we want. Furthermore, technology is not autonomous or deterministic, and, by transforming the internal structure of our urban interfaces (e.g. by changing cities' formats, layouts and social structures), this illusive force can be capitalised upon for positive changes. One scenario that Fathy viewed as a positive in harnessing the potential of technology was that of tele-cities; a critical mass of inhabitants engaged in interactive communication networks where remote services, facilities, and work dominate life. Tele-cities are fundamentally different from traditional urban systems, and therefore require fundamentally different policies, governance systems, and even ways of being.

Mitchell (1999) argues that the capabilities of the underlying urban infrastructure influence cities' functions, and when a new infrastructure system is developed, it is typically overlaid on the existing structures. This superposition can dramatically affect the future response of cities in critical areas of social equity, as well as the long-term sustainability of urban systems. Therefore, there is a need to consider the subsequent immediate effects upon information technology infrastructures, as well as the ways in which interactions with preceding networks produce a joint urban effort. Once again, akin to Fathy, Mitchell places an emphasis on the transition from classic urban design to digital urban design.

In the past, telecommunication inventions such as the telephone and telegraph enabled great leaps in human communication. Thus, one can claim that information networks have classically facilitated 'human interaction at a distance'. Nonetheless, when it comes to the application of information networks to urban systems, the scale of impact is beyond that of merely shortening distances.

To clarify this, let us look at Castells's seminal work, *The Rise of the Network Society* (2009). Before the emergence of digital cities, in studying the complex link between societies and technologies and the impact ICT has in morphing the very fabric of societal systems.

Castells introduced the concept of Network Societies. This concept refers to a space through which flows of information move in a global fashion. Castells (2004) defines network societies as "made of networks in all the key dimensions of social organisations and social practice. In other words, *A network society is a society whose social structure is made of networks powered by microelectronics-based information and communication technologies*".

Structurally speaking, network societies are – to some extent – different to traditional industrial societies. As the definition implies, in network societies the whole global society determines the direction and dynamics of information flows, with societies being no longer fixed on a certain market dynamic, allowing, by means of a relatively minor change, the whole landscape to dramatically shift into a different format. Castells (2009) argues networks constitute the fundamental pattern of life, of all kinds of life, and to function in the era of network societies, there is an urgent need to understand networks' global politics and how networks affect the structural foundations of our societies.

Technological innovations and the emergence of the internet have placed tremendous pressure on the very nature of communications, not just at a societal level, but indeed at the individual level. A massive disorientation in the realm of communications has also resulted in a shift from traditional mass media to a system of horizontal communication networks organised around the internet and wireless communications systems. The transition toward network societies is having a tremendous impact on the future of humanity, and to investigate ways in which such new forms of socialisation can benefit our current systems, for instance urban systems, we must understand how networks influence people and how people's behaviour shapes networks. In this line of thinking, van Bastelaer (1998) argues that digital cities can promote the emergence of so-called "online communities as a virtual space within which citizens interact with information technology".

However, once again, what really matters in these so-called digital cities and the utopia of online communities in a virtual space is a solid and sound grasp of the complex link between people and technology and a comprehensive understanding of digitalisation and its socio-technical, anthropological, cultural, and even spiritual impacts on our lives.

In the original ethos of the digital city, it was seen, defined and sold as the following:

a) Laboratories of integration of multimedia technology within the public space (van Bastelaer, 1998);

b) Information infrastructure, as a communication facility, as a tool for local democracy and participation, as a space for virtual expression and experience, and as a resource for everyday life and for problem solving (Van den Besselaar et al., 1999).

However, when it comes to the practical implications of these cities, studies demonstrate staggering differences between the original ethea of digital cities. In other words, people or users perceive digital cities differently to the ways laid out in experts' definitions and theories.

In studying the inner societal-technological dynamics of digital cities, Van den Besselaar et al. (1999) compared two case studies; those of Parthenay in France and DDS in the Netherlands. In a practical sense, people did not want to use a digital space, virtual space or cyberspace as a replacement for 'online communities'. Instead, what people wanted most was to maintain, reclaim and protect their sense of autonomy.

Moreover, the emergent tech-induced virtual space does not magically eradicate past dynamics. Cyberspace is also not as open as experts would like it to be. Thus, digital cities can become a powerhouse in changing the political space of future cities only once the consideration that experts and people have fundamentally different views on the utility function of this illusive extra dimension of 'cyberspace' is taken into account. This ever-shifting hierarchical gap between inhabitants and local politicians signals changes in two important components of citizenship and governance.

In terms of change of citizenship and application of digital platforms to urban systems, Isin (2002) reviewed changes in citizenship from passivity to the emergence of active citizenship. Active citizenship refers to being active in the local urban life (Mino, 1999), and provides fertile ground for promoting high-level urban goals such as sustainability and social inclusion. Active citizenship was also an element that Van den Besselaar et al. (1999) discovered played a critical role in the ways citizens perceive 'smartness'. Alongside active citizenship, digital cities have further faced the challenge of governance. Due to an increasing level of decentralisation, traditional command-and-control (CC) methods of governance are no longer suitable. Citizens are gaining awareness of issues relating to their rights and choices within the urban space, and henceforth are coming to challenge the old political dimension of the metropolis.

This is an interesting dimension of digital cities that has perhaps inadvertently touched upon the two critical elements of 'public space' and 'citizen participation'. Citizen participation goes back to the anti-Stalinist movement championed by scholars such as Flex Guattari, Guy Debord, Gilles Deleuze, and Michel Foucault. Stalinism refers to the totalitarian way of the Soviet Union, Eastern Europe and China. In addition, the French intellectual Henri Lefebvre was a game-changer through his work against the capitalistic dimension of societies. In his work, Lefebvre put forward the concept of "The Right to the City" as an opportunity to transform classical socialism into an open-ended form of society (Lefebvre, 1996).

In a critical analysis of Lefebvre's work, Purcell (2014) writes that "Lefebvre's work is a Marxism that rejects the state, that maintains itself as an open and evolving project, and that comes to understand itself as more than anything a democratic project, as a struggle by people to shake off the control of capital and the state in order to manage their affairs for themselves".

Lefebvre's analyses are linked to the emerging concept of Smart Cities and the elusive notion of smartness, specifically in his interpretation of socialism. Lefebvre's socialism is not seized and dominated by governments, states and work parties, "It is rather an open project, one that moves us in a direction, toward a horizon beyond the present capitalist and state-bureaucratic society, but whose precise outcomes cannot be fully known". With regard to 'smartness', Lefebvre's work is invaluable, since he was deeply concerned with human life, and advocated for a more holistic understanding of social life in urban systems. This attention to the complexity of urban space and human experience was also noted by Van den Besselaar et al. (1999) in their pursuit of smartness. As highlighted above, people's perception of smartness is very different to experts' definitions. Looking into the existing definitions of Smart Cities, one can nevertheless observe that it is the so-called experts who are currently responsible for defining Smart Cities and shaping dialogue pertaining to smartness.

In conclusion, digital cities have unearthed enlightening truths about emerging urban systems. Cities, citizens, governments, urban infrastructure, and urban communities can no longer be considered as being 'fixed' in space and time. They are continuously changing, and to live in such a state we must learn about networks, self-organisation, citizen awareness, citizen participation, and the transformation of power dynamics. In the next section, I review the definitions of Smart Cities, and continue with the quest to discover how 'smartness' is currently defined, viewed, and operated, and how it can be shifted toward a people-centric smartness.

CHAPTER 2

SHIFTING THE TECHNO-CENTRIC VIEW OF SMARTNESS

With this technological epiphany, it would be a mistake to fail to shift the current comfort zone of the male-dominated and techno-centric vision of smart cities. Looking into projects pertaining to Smart Cities, the intricate critical variables of citizens and government return to the fore. Castells's seminal work, *The Rise of Network Societies* painted a 'Network Reality' in which hierarchies transform into intricate multidimensional connections. So, who is in charge exactly? In short: those who are willing to participate in the creation of something bigger than – and different to – the sum of the individual parts. The whole is bigger than the sum of its parts. The Smart City research domain is largely dominated by experts and technological companies. It is only of late that crucial and subtle aspects of the notion of intelligence, emerging new forms of governance, and the value of citizen science have become evident. I personally became aware of this fact after participating in various Smart City workshops in Brussels and Paris organised by NEXT LEAP, in The Hague organised by the Global Initiative for Ethical Considerations in the Design of Autonomous Systems, and Vienna's Urban Future Conference.

Rethinking Smart Cities with the Theory of Mindfulness Engineering™ facilitates the transition of smart cities from a focus on the Internet of Things and Cloud of Things towards the Internet of People and Cloud of People. Moreover, once the focus of thinking is placed on people and the real meaning of connection, the path for integrating the embedded bits of intelligences, such as emotions, skills, knowledge and ideas, into the underlying philosophy of smart urban design is opened up. Subsequently, cities can begin prioritising different levels of intelligence(s), based on the needs of future generations of smart cities. With such a shift of perspective, thinking and philosophy, the Mindful Smart City Manifesto paints a dynamic, organismic and organic view of reality. The whole is bigger than the sum of its parts.

How to Build a 'We' Space?

To build a WE SPACE, there is a need to question the root of smartness. **"The natural collective intelligence of communities creates an interface with the artificial intelligence of technological platforms"**. The existing conceptualisation of Smart Cities is fundamentally linked to AI literature, and to put forward an alternative point-of-view on conceptualisation of smartness, one must familiarise oneself with the notion of intelligence and its urban-focused implications. Most AI scientists define intelligence based on the implicit conditions of an agent's ability to adapt to a wide range of environments, and to learn from and interact with its environment(s) should environmental conditions shift or agent's objects change (Legg and Hutter, 2007).

Within Smart Cities literature, both within the definition and within the analytical frameworks, very few have questioned the *kind* of intelligence upon which Smart Cities of the future should be built. Consequently, the majority of smartness ideologies are technologically oriented. Rarely do we see scholars advocate for cities that are based on implicit dimensions or soft facets of intelligent existence, such as kindness, compassion, understanding, awareness, mindfulness, tolerance, curiosity, serendipity, beauty, appreciation, gratitude, self-mastery, self-knowledge, or self-actualisation. To uncover the difference between the expert view of Smart Cities and the citizen view of Smart Cities, I developed a template for the kinds of questions that can help practitioners to widen their perspective on the specific role technology can play in creating a more inclusive, diverse and mindful notion of intelligence.

Let's Break the Monopoly of the Data-Driven Smart Cities

There is a space and appetite for proposing an alternative approach toward smart cities, a vision of cities as unique systems with different needs, priorities and smartnesses. To do this, I propose the analytical lens of Mindfulness Engineering™. What is Mindfulness Engineering, and where does it come from?

I originally developed the theory of Mindfulness Engineering™ during my PhD on the subject of resilience of complex adaptive systems. The theory connects together perspectives on resilience from diverse and largely disconnected research domains, and maps these onto the resilience of infrastructure and communities (Beigi, 2015). It asserts that physical (e.g. the built environment) and social (e.g. political, economic and legal) infrastructure systems are created to meet the needs and wants of people and communities. These infrastructure systems need to be in connection with the environmental and ecological systems within which they exist, with which they interact, and from which they draw energies and resources. Such interconnection will, in turn, promote the interconnection of individuals' and communities' behaviours and interactions with the environmental and ecological systems. Mindfulness Engineering™ attempts to explain and frame the complexity and interdependency between infrastructures, ecosystems and societies. It places an emphasis on the role of humans, and their adaptation styles and methods, in shaping the overall system's resilient properties and capabilities, such as thriving in the face of adversity. Mindfulness Engineering™ provides an interdisciplinary unit of analysis of resilience, termed the Resilient Agent (RA), which spans across various domains and disciplines, and links the concept of resilience to the future of urbanisation. With the increasing rate of urbanisation across the world, and enhanced utilisation of the internet and data, the building of Resilient Living Spaces (RLS) and Resilient Interfaces (RI) must become an integral part of the future of engineering. Mindfulness Engineering™ defines Mindfulness as being in the present moment and being conscious of everything from a variety of perspectives (including historical and future-oriented) across the environmental, ecological, social and technological domains, when creating new concepts and distinctions in the process of satisfying human needs and wants. It explicitly seeks to avoid automatic, 'mindless', thought processes. In other words, it emphasises clear, purposeful, cognitive functioning and learning. I apply the template of Mindfulness Engineering™ (X-Agent, X-Living Space, X-Interface) by taking into account that urban systems are one class of complex adaptive systems, and therefore, in order to make them smart or resilient, one must understand the underlying template of these systems. To analyse the behaviour and evolutionary patterns of complex adaptive systems, it is essential to understand these systems as a combination of parts, embedded in ecosystems, with interdependent relationships with one another and creating an interface with their surroundings within which information related to part-whole interactions continuously flows. I believe the existing scientific literature does not have terminology of equal power to that of Mindfulness that can unite visions across the field. The concept of Mindfulness has more recently been brought to the attention of the digital community under the notion of Digital Mindfulness which, as the phrase implies, is the mindful use of technology. This terminology has largely been developed due to an ever-increasing trend of digital addiction. This terminology is also used for smart platforms that promote the practice of Mindfulness. In this Manifesto, I will apply the term 'Mindfulness' in a manner consistent with the original usage within Mindfulness Engineering™ described above, because I believe that this definition provokes a dialogue on the community-technology balance. Additionally, in this Manifesto I attempt to bring attention to the other forms of intelligence, such as emotions, skills, creativities, knowledge, empathy, compassion, etc.

CHAPTER 3

WHY RE-THINK SMART CITIES WITH MINDFULNESS ENGINEERING?

We cannot build new systems with the old way of thinking. Mindfulness Engineering™ is about building for the emergence of a growth-oriented mindset. A Resilient, Mindful and Smart Citizen needs to have a growth-oriented mindset that interprets change as an opportunity for learning, evolution and growth. Technology can be seen as a catalyst that paves novel pathways for humanity's flourishing in this process.

Mindfulness Engineering™ aims to challenge the classical take of engineering disciplines with regard to adaptation to shocks and stresses, such as man-made or natural disasters, demands of new technologies, changes of climates, and collapses of economic systems. In the classical, traditional view of engineering, shocks and stressors exist in isolation from the social, psychological, cultural and behavioural dimensions of the design methodology. Therefore, such a view fails to provide systemic solutions for a sustainable adaptation to future shocks, or for building resilient systems and human-centred integration of technology into human lives.

Mindfulness Engineering™ attempts to fill the gaps by linking aspects of neuroscience such as Mindfulness and awareness into the world of design. With regard to Smart Cities, given the multidimensional space of the Smart Cities domain, from definition, through conceptualisation, to the operationalization phase, Mindfulness Engineering™ provides a fresh perspective: it contributes to the rethinking process of designing smarter cities and realignment with human-centric values. The majority of Smart City definitions centred around ICT platforms and the notions of 'intelligence and smartness' are often misjudged.

With Mindfulness Engineering™, I take a systemic approach to Smart Cities, and view cities as a mixture of a diverse range of complex adaptive systems, namely socio-ecological, socio-technical and psycho-social systems. A social system is a result of aggregation and self-organisation of human endeavours, and it clusters within hub-like entities, such as cities.

Energy and resources from the surrounding environments and systems are in continuous demand by cities, much in a similar way to biological organisms. With this (inter) dependency upon external elements, cities develop emergent characteristics such as resilience, sustainability, liveability and smartness. These characteristics emerge from spontaneous dynamics between local interactions and sub-processes that run through and across them, as well as the continuous and mutual adaptation of society, ecosystems, technical systems, technology and other systems to a changing environment.

Unlike the contemporary label of Smart Cities – which is focused on ICT platforms – Mindfulness Engineering™ considers smart cities as interfaces. Interfaces for understanding the intricate interdependence and interconnection of diverse potentialities. This means that the interface between technology and pre-existing urban structures opens up a completely new dimension for imagining cohesive living places.

From a Mindfulness Engineering™ perspective, infrastructure systems are extensions of natural systems, and, similar to the evolution of biological systems, urban infrastructure systems have gone through evolutionary phases; we build bridges because of the need to connect places, we build roads and stations due to the needs and demands placed on our cities.

These morphing behaviours, continuous adaptations to the changes of external and internal environments, are intelligent, meaning they manifest as a result of human cognitive capacities and learning behaviours. Therefore, philosophically speaking, smartness is not a matter of an absence or existence of ICT platforms or integration of sensors. Cities are already smart. The question is to what extent the bits and pieces of subtle intelligences such as knowledge, kindness, diversity, learning, etc. can be extended into ICT-Smartness.

This is linked to our conceptual, epistemological and ontological understanding of the notion of 'intelligence'. Similar to what we see in education, our theory of intelligence needs expansion. Take, for instance, the Theory of Multiple Intelligences (Gardner, 2000), which states that unlike the classical logical-mathematical emphasis of IQ, humans process information in myriad ways. For example, while some are savvy with mathematical-logical gifts, there are linguistic, interpersonal, intra-personal, musical, bodily kinaesthetic, visual-spatial intelligences, whereby a whole new experience of life is created. Having this perspective on the nature of intelligence and how it can affect people's livelihoods, choices and experiences when thinking about Smart Cities, it is overly simplistic to define 'smartness' only through an ICT lens, or what experts, programmers, politicians, big companies such as IBM, Google, Cisco and similar, would define as 'smart'.

How Does Mindfulness Engineering™ Transform Smart Cities into Mindful Smart Cities?

When asking about the meaning of a Smart City, the Mindful Smart City Manifesto argues that Smartness is not about how we connect objects through the fluid platform of the internet, rather Smartness is about our ability to use technology as a resource, as a potentiality to bring forth highest form of intelligence that is self-actualisation and sense of agency.

To use technology in service of higher human needs, and in support of a global democratic urban reality, the Mindful Smart City Manifesto calls on people, communities, experts, and all parties involved in integration of ICT into urban affairs, to investigate how automatisation of urban systems alters human feelings and emotional realities. In practical terms, technology should not be used as an alternative to real, meaningful relationships. Additionally, with the massive flow of data, protecting citizens' privacy has to be the defining moral compass of future-generation Smart Cities.

Let's Look at C7 of the Mindful Smart City Manifesto

C7. Mindfulness Engineering™ views Smart Cities as a space of possibility with these goals: Sustaining Resilience of Social-Ecological-Technical Systems, Customising Innovative

Growth and Evolution Trends, and Harnessing the Cognitive Capacities of Resilient Agents for Management of Resilience.

Mindfulness Engineering™ views Mindful Smart Cities as WE SPACES. Mindful Smart Cities are about co-creation, co-evolution and enrichment of human lives. Another way in which Mindfulness Engineering™ transforms Smart Cities into Mindful Smart Cities is by encouraging a *gender-balanced vision of intelligence, a human-centric view of technology, an inclusivity mindset, and, last but not least, by categorically emphasising the non-programmability of the Human Becoming Experience.*

As a resilience scientist, I believe that resilience plays a critical role in designing the future of the Smart City. Granted, in this Manifesto I continue to advocate for building resilience. In this resilience-centric point of view, Mindful Smart Cities are complex systems including both social-ecological and socio-technical systems. An element of resilience is sustainable development and given that cities contribute to a large share of environmental changes, societal transformations as well as economic growth, it is necessary to integrate the 17 sustainable goals into the future agendas of Smart Cities.

As I discussed in C6 of this Manifesto, unlike the contemporary label of Smart Cities, which is focused on ICT platforms, Mindfulness Engineering™ considers Smart Cities as interfaces. I originally coined the Resilient Living Space concept in relation to urban systems.

From the vantage point of resilience, the Mindful Smart City has to be a resilient system, meaning its infrastructure systems have to be resilient in the face of shocks and have to be continuously able to sustain citizens' needs for energy and resources without degrading the resilience of its supportive ecological systems.

Customising Growth and Evolutions Trends

Citizens of a smart city are *intrinsically motivated* to share their experiences of citizenship with each other and to self-organise solutions related to the use of physical and nonphysical elements of the city from a bottom-up perspective. These processes of sharing and exchange utilise the *cultural identity* of the city as a complex adaptive system, and empower the process of progression toward sustainable outcomes that are in harmony with nature. In the Resilient Living Space framework, these outcomes are achieved by means of the collective efforts of Resilient Agents to continuously avoid unwanted states (i.e., identifying the early signs of critical transitions that can lead to catastrophic collapse) and shift away from such undesirable scenarios.

Harnessing Cognitive Capacities of Resilient Agents for Managing Resilience

Citizens of a smart city are motivated to take a responsible and system level view of their role in the city. Doing so, 'shared awareness' emerges as one of the many fundamental features of resilience and sustainable development. The interactions between Resilient, Mindful and Smart Agents and Resilient Living Spaces combine the dynamics of social-ecological, and infrastructure resilience, and movement of social agents as logical actors in the physical and nonphysical pathways of cities.

The outcome of this linkage gives rise to smartness as an emergent property of 21st-century cities. A city can be described as 'smart' when it enjoys a sufficient degree of autonomy through the harmoniously crafted management strategies of its users. While ICT is a necessary part of the process of becoming smart, it is not sufficient on its own.

Designing Mindful Smart Cities with Mindfulness Engineering™

What Is a Mindful Smart Living Space?

A Smart Living Space is a platform for changing the world into a better place and reducing its exploitation. And for this to happen, the focus of smartification has to shift towards looking at people and the connection between machines and humans as an additional subset of the Smart Living Space. Our current take on Smart Cities is a cerebral take on the properties of intelligence such as calculation, efficiency, problem solving and resource allocation. However, if we take a more realistic and pragmatic understanding of the nature of life *per se*, it is evident that each of us 'already' cultivates a certain type of cognitive map within our minds. The cognitive map might be hidden from others – and even from ourselves – but it dictates the degree of smartness of our choices, our attitude toward life, and our outlook on global challenges. Mindfulness Engineering™ illustrates that prior to making any judgement on the impact of ICT platforms on cities and how they can make cities smart, we can promote Smart Living in our own intimate space of the self. The self is taken as our internal frame of reference, the common denominator that we carry regardless of our locality. Our internal self hence becomes a smart guiding compass, directing our behaviours.

This is connected to the existing gap of saturation of the imagination apparatus of classical architecture, urban planning, engineering, technologist mindset, that is present in current future smart cities practices. Having practiced Taoism, meditation and silence meditations for more than a decade, I came to notice that a peaceful future can emerge only if our minds go beyond what is superimposed on them as limits and obstacles. The relevance of this is that, when reading literature, an ideology persists that technology can somehow magically help societies buffer future uncertainties.

However, with this mindset, technology will merely act as a sticking plaster remedy for old school control systems.

What Is a Mindful Smart Agent?

In conceptualising Smart Cities, scholars have already proposed systems such as the smart economy and smart environment. Within the Mindfulness Engineering™ viewpoint, humans are complex systems with inherent embedded learning capabilities. Through this learning mechanism, they adapt to the changes of the external environment and self-organise. This viewpoint sees humans as already highly smart systems. Therefore, what they need is not greater smartification through an ICT platform, but rather greater alignment and steering toward becoming better at managing their already existing intelligences.

Technology envelops us and surrounds us with an information bubble. How does this bubble burst?

We can enable people to seek a more meaningful life and encourage them to see themselves as a small but beautiful part of the Earth's system. What would be the value of becoming smart if our collective mind and attitude toward shared risks and challenges, and our responsibilities toward living life fully, are held in the hands of something outside our own power?

This line of argument looks favourably upon the emerging theme of Active Citizenship. Such citizenship seeks a shift in our perception of the world, a paradigm shift in how we place and actualise our individual egos within the complex web of relationships we share throughout the fluid course of our citizenship. Carlo Ratti (2013) emphasises on a similar argument as the following: "...A Smart City isn't made by people just responding to inputs, but by citizens performing an essential role: the leading role in the process of data collection and sharing. Connected citizens are the engine of urban change in the city of the future".

What Is a Mindful Smart Interface?

Perhaps one of the most smart interfaces that we have is that of our own bodies and Mother Nature. All information that permeates into our bodies is shared, and it is this 'smart sharing' that shapes our reaction and colours our experiences. A hallmark of well-balanced sharing is a sense of wellbeing that is generated by balanced and intelligent trade-offs between the human ecosystem and its surrounding spaces. In developing

Mindfulness Engineering™, my frame of reference for a Smart City is Mother Nature. Looking at natural ecosystems, for instance trees, one can see that nature is a Smart City in its own right, but of a kind of intelligence that is radically different to that of the classical cerebral definition of intelligence. Nature is intelligent due to the highly synergic and cooperative interconnections that species share across various scales. With this Gaia-inspired Smart City design mindset, Technological Singularity, a critical point over which artificial intelligence (AI) will take over human civilisations causing a fundamental shift in their evolution, can be seen as an opportunity for empowering people and enriching the human experience of awareness by making cities smarter (Shanahan, 2012).

The Mindful Smart City: a Space of Possibilities

More than half of the world's population now lives in cities, and it is estimated that by 2050 the increase in urban population of both developing and developed countries will have resulted in significant changes to land utilisation practices. With most urbanisation occurring upon land under some form of stress, such as arid land, and considering the increase in frequency and intensity of natural and man-made disasters, a major global challenge is that of understanding and predicting how changes in social organisations and dynamics resulting from urbanisation will impact the interaction between nature, societies and technology.

Smart Cities provide a potent platform for understanding the interface between these complex and interconnected systems. At the same time, Resilience Theory emphasises the importance of understanding the trade-offs, learning and self-organisation, and feedback across various scales.

A Resilient Smart Mindful Living Space provides opportunities/alternatives for the previously introduced concept of the Resilient Smart Mindful Agent to harness its attention in order to facilitate the processing of signals that would otherwise pass unnoticed. In short, while the Resilient, Mindful and Smart Agent does the 'Resilience Thinking'; The Resilient Smart Living Space 'navigates' the Resilient Mindful and Smart Agent.

Navigation of social-ecological-technical systems means a degree of responsibility of social agents in shaping the outcomes of management insight, combined with a desire for long-term profit rather than short-term fixes. The evolution of the Resilient Living Space is in the direction of 'Smarter, and More Mindful, Living Spaces'.

I formulate the concept of Smart Cities as an aspiration for the emergence of higher orders MEMES, equivalent to genes, in the mental landscape of Resilient Agents/citizens. A meme transfers ideas from one mind to another. In the digital world, we face an exaggerated degree of meme-sharing, which can lead to what is termed the 'information rich – wisdom poor' paradox. The RLS views a city as an aggregate and emergent super-object that is built by the conscious acts of its dwellers.

Citizens Have a Right to the City. Citizens also Have a Right to the Design Of Cities

Indeed, Citizens have a right to the application of artificial intelligence and the integration process of ICT into cities. This incorporates the rights, characteristics, features and qualities that civil society should expect from living in a Mindful Smart City. This Mindful Smart City will provide opportunities for gleaning insights from the flow of data and information entering its mind-body system. It is expected that, by applying the ethos of this Manifesto, citizens will be able to restore, reclaim and protect their sense of autonomy, spontaneity, creativity, spirituality and freedom of experience. Citizens of a Mindful Smart City should have high levels of agency and agency thinking, resulting in the emergence of a 'High Hope' personality type. Hope enables better decision-making in the face of uncertainties. A Mindful Smart City must encourage dreaming for a better future. Living in a Mindful Smart City is also about learning about evolution and, by acquiring a strategic and visionary adaptive capacity, the ability to manage resilience potential in times of change. Citizens of a Mindful Smart City must be encouraged to transform daily stressors into resources for enhancing their social-ecological-technical memory. The gain from shocks enables the Smart Mindful Agent to undergo smooth metamorphosis processes when the conditions are no longer tenable (i.e. anti-fragility). This smooth transition out of disorder enables the Smart Mindful Agent to achieve post-traumatic growth.

Post-traumatic growth is marked by a significant alteration of one's philosophy of life after being exposed to psychological seismic waves such as spousal loss, physical disabilities, and other life crises. This special type of growth results from five factors namely; (1) greater appreciation of life and changed sense of priorities; (2) warmer, more intimate relationships with others; (3) a greater sense of personal strength; (4) recognition of new possible paths for one's life; and (5) spiritual development.

The Resilient, Mindful and Smart Agents consider themselves a part of a whole. This means an ability to see the bigger picture, and, in turn, that technology serves as a means to enhance citizens' consciousness, awareness and collective evolution.

CHAPTER 4

IT'S ABOUT SMARTFULNESS®

SMARTFULNESS® is a gender-balanced view of AI, technology and digitalisation that brings forth a Mindful Smart City Spirit. SMARTFULNESS® seeks connections that create something more valuable for everyone. It is a spirit of creating win-win ecosystems. Our traditional view of 'smartness' is heavily gender-biased, with an overwhelming degree of ideas coming from male, white, privileged backgrounds. A truly smart city fights against this gender imbalance. A Mindful Smart City achieves smartness as a result of diversities of views on the nature of intelligence and technology, and their roles within and upon human life. Women, in both scientific and private technological companies, represent a very small percentage of thought leaders. This chapter demonstrates the power of female leadership in the tech industry, and narrates an entirely different vision for the Smart City. I argue that to make cities smart, one must follow these steps:

PROCESS OF GENERATING SMARTFULNESS

SMARTFULNESS® is a gender-balanced view of AI, technology and digitalisation that builds Mindful Smart City Spirit. SMARTFULNESS® seeks connections that create something more valuable for everyone. It is a spirit of creating win-win ecosystems.

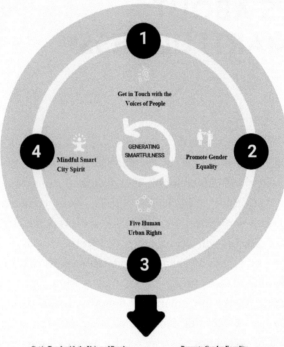

Get in Touch with the Voices of People

Highlight under-represented communities, such as immigrants and women, and those who are excluded from existing Smart Cities ideologies.

Promote Gender Equality

Men and women use technology differently and hold different views on technology. But this difference is mutually inclusive. Henceforth, there is a huge creative value in having both male and female views on technology.

Mindful Smart City Spirit

Mindful Smart Cities is about co-creation, co-evolution and enrichment of human lives.

Five Human Urban Rights

The Right to the Smart City.
The Right to Design.
The Right to Technology.
The Right to Information.
The Right to Becoming.

Get in Touch with the Voices of People

Foulon's observation brings me to a memory. In October 2015, I participated in one of the biggest European Union-organised technology events in Lisbon. I remember very vividly a dramatic absence of women in technology and IT. Intimidated by my own presence, I had a conversation with one of the biggest French IT suppliers who stated that he found it sad that they only meet very few women at such large events. I am not sure whether this is because of cultural drivers, or because women have never been encouraged or relied upon as IT solution generators. Additionally, during the literature review phase, I was shocked by the extent to which the vision of the AI and tech industry is male-formed. In another event, on the Morality and Ethics of AI, organised in the Netherlands, I was among the panel of speakers. And in that panel, the importance of feminine qualities such as compassion or empathy was missing from the agenda. After attending several events on Smart Cities across Europe, the Middle East and Asia, it became evident to me that the best approach to uncover what people want from ICT platforms is to speak with individuals who are already interacting with people. Soon, I discovered: "The majority of existing platforms are highly technical, male-oriented, and predominantly designed by White Europeans".

I was deeply affected by the terrorist attacks in Brussels. So, I decided to investigate how today's technological interconnectivity contributed to these unfortunate incidents.

Brussels is unlike any other city in the world in which I have lived so far. Part of this difference is that Brussels is a very fragmented city, with 19 different communes, with only one postcode, 1000, acting as a common point. You rarely see communities of one commune connecting to other districts, for example to go for dinner. They do not really move from their commune. Molenbeek is very Moroccan-oriented. Ixelles, it is definitely French. Uccle, another municipality, is predominantly French. Saint Gilles is predominantly populated by the Portuguese and Spanish. In other words, every commune is organised like a cultural identity. Another stark difference between Brussels and other cities is linguistic diversity and division.

While the case of Brussels and its complexity has motivated me to provide a new way of thinking in the Smart City domain, the biggest motivation to write this Manifesto was to address the challenge of gender equality in the tech industry and to highlight the degree to which under-represented communities, such as immigrants and women, are excluded from existing Smart Cities ideologies.

To dive deeper into these issues, I decided to speak to one of the co-founders of MolenGeek, a Brussels based Smart City platform. Located in Molenbeek, MolenGeek is an ideation space organised within a co-working space, where young entrepreneurs come to work on their projects, network and share experiences. MolenGeek is also a coding school which opened its doors on 1 March 2017, in partnership with

Bruxelles Formation, Université Libre de Bruxelles (ULB), Google and Samsung.

The notions of what a Smart City theoretically could be and what it can be in practice are radically different. After decades of working in the technical industry, I felt, I knew where the root of the current techno-centric view of smart cities resided. The majority of existing platforms are highly technical, male-oriented, and predominantly designed by White European males. In addition, technology and platforms designed by women tend to differ from those designed by men. A female approach to technology could translate into a different output. The message is clear: men and women use technology differently and hold different views on technology. But this difference is rather mutually inclusive. Henceforth, there is a huge creative value in having both male and female views on technology.

The Issue of Gender Equality in Start-Up Ecosystems

Inspired by the vision to give voice to women in the digital space and to make a difference in the tech industry, I connected with Julie Foloun. Foulon founded Girleek in 2011. Girleek soon turned into the main Belgian technology blog for women and girls. From this vision, Foulon came to lead the largest tech community in Belgium called BetaGroup. At the time, BetaGroup was one of the biggest tech communities in Brussels, with more than more than 8,000 members. Overall, around 5,000-6,000 people came and pitched their ideas to the community and, in exchange, they were able to receive feedback, meet with investors, network, and maybe sometimes hire specialist developers, and so on. Foloun noticed that the regional fragmentation and division of Brussels is not conducive to the cross-connection of ideas. This would translate into the formation of a profile of those present at BetaGroup: middle-class, upper-class, people with higher education, and, again, few women and few students. This profile was consistent; despite the fact that some of these events were organised at the university, only seven percent of the BetaGroup community was composed of students. The ecosystems of these male-dominated start-ups were also very technical. This highly White male techno-centric point of view is less evident in other universities and start-ups across the world. With this observation, Foulon met a Belgian Moroccan entrepreneur, Ibrahim, and together they organised the first technology event in Molenbeek to test whether people would consider participating.

How Can We Create Technological Ecosystems that Enable Authentic Human Connection?

After observing the gender gap in the Smart City ecosystem of Brussels, and discovering the male-dominated reality of start-up culture across Europe, I realised that the root of these issues goes beyond the scope of information technology. The message was loud and clear: diversity was missing from the regular Brussels tech meetings.

The Mindful Smart City Manifesto aims to change this pervasive pattern by providing a platform upon which to build the required inviting ecosystem. Aesthetics of Design matter. These are elements of the Right to Design, which will be discussed further below. To foster greater diversity and encourage citizens' participation, a welcoming and safe atmosphere is needed. This brings me to the importance of designing Smart Living Spaces with an ethos of diversity at their heart.

Case studies such as MolenGeek made me realise that the template of the Smart Living Space is a general model for the emergence of smartness. By paying attention to the subtle elements of culture and gender gaps, this start-up has transformed into a melting pot, a cultural space unlike the regular tech ecosystem in Brussels.

To create ecosystems that enable authentic connection between people, there is also a need for an emotionally educated leader around whom the community feels safe to explore the new frontiers of science. The majority of current technological events *always have the same kind of profile (White, male, higher education). But what about everyone else?*

The Mindful Smart City Manifesto aims to change this pervasive pattern by raising awareness of the inaccessibility of current technological jargon, which distances itself from locals. But let us look at some of the real cases in which the current White, male, English-speaking technology culture and mindset isolates citizens from their legitimate Right to the City, and the right to be a part of the development of their urban system.

Extracted from my visit to MolenGeek:

"KBS Brussels is the biggest incubator in Belgium. They have six locations. And hundreds of start-ups began there. So I was leading the incubators in Brussels. And, one day, a young woman, M, she had great ideas, she was a designer. She was doing special dresses and she was also doing workshops on wearing a veil for women who lose their hair after cancer, you know. She had great ideas and so on. She had a project and she wanted to be incubated. So, I welcomed her to KBC. And during one morning, I was excited and introducing her to other start-ups and, you know, I was trying to show her that she has a role to play in this ecosystem. The first thing that she did after the meeting was to call Ibrahim to say: No that's not for me. Julie was nice but this ecosystem, KBC, is not for me. Because she was not feeling confident. Because everybody was speaking English, and because everybody was speaking about complex concepts such as Blockchain... so maybe she did not understand what was going on, and for her it created a distance.

And we arrived at the conclusion that most of the young people, or most people, in a district like Molenbeek don't go to institutions and organisations for entrepreneurs because they do not recognise themselves in those organisations. It is not the same code, it is not the same, you know, attitude. And, for most of them they are not confident enough, and probably if they receive feedback, they would think it is because of them instead of because of the project! And, that is one reason we started MolenGeek, and straight away it was a success. And, actually by putting things together, putting incubators together in Molenbeek, because Ibrahim is from Molenbeek, and with a nice furniture and with all the facilities to help people to start their projects, straight away a lot of young people without an academic background or IT background or skills came to MolenGeek to develop their own projects."

Citizen Participation Is at the Heart of the Mindful Smart City Manifesto

Therefore, I make it clear that in order to promote a cross-connection of skills and ideas and social mobility, there is a need to shift to a democratic model of governance. In short, designers, people, tech developers and all parties involved in developing the agenda of future Smart Cities must become mindful of the power of loose hierarchies. Cities are about people, and so are start-ups. They are the engines of creativity and innovation. They are the emerging places where a revolution in human development will take place.

Reflecting on the MolenGeek case, I realised that, in a way, MolenGeek is a kind of Smart City in itself, because power was given to the people by giving access to new technologies and entrepreneurship to everybody.

They could find a way to break the barriers of social mobility and gender inequality in the tech world. And, today, thanks to the training, workshops and events they organise, they have developed their outreach to new members, called *MolenGeeks*. Today, these members can attend tech meet-ups feeling comfortable and qualified.

The story behind MolenGeek raises an important point about the power of connecting like-minded people and self-actualisation from diverse backgrounds in generating creative capital. One of the two co-founders, Julie, has a university-level education in finance, while the other, Ibrahim, dropped out of school when he was 13 years old. Regardless, these young people broke free from the classical labour market by becoming freelancers. They embraced their inner entrepreneurs and dared to develop their own companies, consciously creating the kind of digital world in which they want to live and belong.

The Mindful Smart City Manifesto views the future of work as a matter of vocational calling rather than an obligation to be a part of economic systems. People are increasingly becoming aware of the potential of ICT platforms as an avenue to emancipation and creating their own jobs. The Mindful Smart City Manifesto pays attention to these changes in people's awareness of work and economic systems, seeing them as an inspiring axes for developing the future Smart City.

Fostering the Formation of Smartfulness®

Below I present the outcomes of the discussion group at MolenGeek. The key outcome of this discussion group was strong evidence to suggest a different functional reality of a Smart Hub from what is perceived by the scientific literature as 'Smart'. At the MolenGeek co-sharing space, 'smartness' is not a fixed measurable mathematical variable. None of the pre-existing models of a Smart City could be used to describe the experiential reality of life at MolenGeek. People do not immediately adopt technology. People's idea of connectedness is linked to accessibility of technological platforms and the degree to which these platforms are human-centric. The social sensitivity of the developers at MolenGeek has enabled them to connect with the community. Additionally, MolenGeek takes an ecological approach to technology. This means that, early on, the start-up identified that, in order for them to make a difference, they would need to merge with the spirit and culture of the space. In essence, the success of the start-up is a result of its early investment in non-ICT variables such as cultural diversity of the place, high percentage of unemployed youth population, and their own expertise as to the pitfalls of traditional Smart City ecosystems.

Current Smart City Developers Do Not Pay Attention to the Fluid Nature of Information

The Mindful Smart City Manifesto advocates for maximising coordination in complex systems through mechanisms such as embedded self-organisation; *stigmergy*. Stigmergy is a mechanism of indirect coordination in which the trace left by an action upon a medium stimulates subsequent action. Stigmergy is a widely known and commonly studied phenomenon within social insect colonies. The concept is also commonly applied in web communities and robotics. Concepts such as stigmergy provide a different take on the nature of intelligence and the mechanism(s) by which intelligent behaviour emerges in networked systems. The Mindful Smart City Manifesto takes an organic view on the nature of intelligence by viewing it as an act of coordination between people. This view of smartness as connected mechanisms of coordination opens a fertile avenue for Active Citizenship and Participatory Governance. My visits to MolenGeek and other start-ups – which will be discussed later – highlight the need for triangulation of the scientific understanding of smartness with the local reality of translation of smartness.

Locals view and interpret 'Smart' as something beyond what ICT platforms could ever provide them with. People want to feel connected to something meaningful. People want their voice to be heard, rather than to be provided with soulless machines, sensors, applications and social engineering.

In short, people *recognise* 'the value of ICT-enabled spaces' when they *feel* they have been included in something that has the right balance of newness and connection to the past.

A lack of interconnection of ICT-enabled platforms with the emotional, psychological, cultural and spiritual aspects of life, combined with the inherent uncertainty brought about by digitalisation, are all areas that require collective thinking. Henceforth, to create Mindful Smart Cities, this Manifesto further calls for building a value proposition for non-ICT related elements such as cultural diversity, and implicit and abstract components such as love, compassion, empathy, kindness, and mindfulness.

A Mindful Smart City Needs a Smart and Mindful Spirit and Consciousness

Conceptually speaking, a city is made up of a dense agglomeration of energy and matter in the form of people and assets (Glaeser, 1998). Technically speaking, however, a city is a complex system in a dynamic state of flux. Therefore, cities are more than just energetic realities and 'their future changes as future changes'. This is the first time in human history that we are forced to accept that imagining the future is a futile effort; the future unfolds on its own terms and we need to keep adapting on a constant basis. Maybe it is the first time that the Spirit of Time, the Zeitgeist, is calling us to adopt a different mindset, a mindset that appreciates change, adaptation and resilience. The call of the Zeitgeist to avoid silo thinking and generalisation, and to welcome and embrace change can further be identified in the emerging conceptualisation of 21st-century cities that place an emphasis on 'abilities of cities to attract people' and 'economic management of the costs of moving creative workforce, ideas, know-how, and knowledge'. This Manifesto invites the future generation of researchers, designers, urban theorists, artists and people to ponder these questions:

- What does 'smart' mean for your people?
- What is the call of the Zeitgeist in your City?
- How can you encourage a more WE SPACE-centred design philosophy, as opposed to a Technology-focused design philosophy?
- Are you listening to the voices of people?
- What can you do to balance the gender inequality and gap in the Tech World?
- What kind of power dynamics are at place in your city?
- How can power be given back to the people?

CHAPTER 5

THE MINDFUL SMART CITY

Mindfulness Engineering™ views Smart Cities as an opportunity to extend Mindfulness and to design Mindful Smart Cities as WE SPACE(s). The Mindful Smart City is about the organic production of knowledge. This means that the application of technological devices should feed the human mind and soul as much as it feeds developers' economic gains. Essentially, the future of our society depends on the posing of a number of philosophical questions, asking humans to become aware of – and take responsibility for – the state of the world, take on an active role in making this world a better place, become more inclusive, become more 'WE' and less 'I'. This means moving toward an Earth Gaia Consciousness.

What Is a "We Space"?

A WE SPACE is an intersubjective space, an interface to explore possibilities of becoming more. A WE SPACE is a space of refinement, a space of procreation, a space of inclusion, a space for healing tensions and conflicts. A WE SPACE is a space that includes and respects the five sub-categories of human urban rights, namely The Right to the City, The Right to Design, The Right to Technology, The Right to Information and The Right to Becoming.

The Right to the City

The Right to the City finds its origins in the works of Henry Lefebvre, and is a call to make cities about people. The right to the city of the 1990s did not predict the emergence of so-called Smart Cities, or cities that would be heavily reliant on ICT platforms for their day-to-day functioning. David Harvey defines the Right to the City as: "far more than the individual liberty to access urban resources: it is a right to change ourselves by changing the city. It is, moreover, a common rather than an individual right since this transformation inevitably depends upon the exercise of a collective power to reshape the processes of urbanisation. The freedom to make and remake our cities and ourselves is, I want to argue, one of the most precious yet most neglected of our human rights" (Harvey, 2008). Building on this vital construction of modern urbanisation, in this Manifesto I propose four other important rights, i.e., the Right to Design, the Right to Technology, the Right to Information and the Right to Becoming. Each of these rights marks an important aspect of the future of smart cities. The Right to Design connects

MINDFUL SMART CITY FIVE HUMAN URBAN RIGHTS

A Mindful Smart City is built from a vantage point and consciousness of a WE SPACE. A WE SPACE is a space where we share our humanity as opposed to our data. This WE SPACE is filled with pockets of awareness of the collective Five Human Urban Rights of Smart City Citizenship. WE SPACE is about reframing the way we see the world.

01 THE RIGHT TO SMART CITY

The Right to Smart is an extension of the right to the City originated by Henry Lefebvre and is a call to make cities about people. A Mindful Smart City is defined as a "WE SPACE". A WE SPACE is a space where we share our humanity as opposed to our data. Data is a by-product of our current technological capabilities.

02 THE RIGHT TO DESIGN

The Right to Design connects people to urban developers and technological stakeholders. THE RIGHT TO DESIGN means cities must become visually aesthetic and cognitively stimulating. They must become places for promoting creative thinking, entrepreneurship, compassion and resilience.

03 THE RIGHT TO TECHNOLOGY

The Right to Technology connects ICT developers to the people. the Right to Technology is about going beyond pleasure principles as the driving force of human behaviour. The Right to Technology is about bringing awareness and consciousness into the digital world.

04 THE RIGHT TO INFORMATION

The Right to Information puts the power in the hands of people. To make room for the mindful in smart, an emphasis should be placed on methods which direct information flows toward sustainability and knowledge. Technological companies are responsible for attempting to shift communities towards mindful interactions with data rather than promoting addictive patterns.

05 THE RIGHT TO BECOMING

The Right to Becoming reminds everyone that ICT-driven cities must focus on human self-actualisation and empowerment. The Right to Becoming is about becoming Mindfully Smart in the Globalised, Urbanised and Digitalised (GUD) World. Right to Becoming means Mindfulness can be extended into technological platforms and manifest itself as SMARTFULNESS®. SMARTFULNESS® means Holding Space for Others.

people to urban developers and technological stakeholders, The Right to Technology connects ICT developers to the people, The Right to Information puts the power in the hands of people, and The Right to Becoming reminds everyone that ICT-driven cities must focus on human self-actualisation and empowerment. The Right to Becoming connects directly to the spirit of Mindful Smart Cities: Technology connects but it is the human heart and consciousness that matters.

What Is the Right to Design?

There is a part of existence as a whole, humanity included, that cannot be programmed by Artificial Intelligence, simply as a virtue of it being artificial. This is the thinking behind The Right to Design. With The Right to Design, cities become more than artefacts. The Right to Design directly connects the brain's language to the features of urban landscape. Human-centred urban layout as well as density are all design elements that should replace current smart city design protocols. Further, The Right to Design means cities must become visually aesthetic and cognitively stimulating. They must become places for promoting creative thinking, entrepreneurship, compassion and resilience.

With the ever-increasing flow of information, our inner state of equilibrium is continuously pushed and pulled. We are challenged to find ways to stay away from this rapidly expanding 'Notification Universe'. Our behaviour is becoming increasingly faster-paced, and we believe that we are losing something precious along the way. Granted, with Mindfulness Engineering™ in Action, I endeavoured to create a place for digital literacy and challenge 'our collective behaviour on-the-go'.

Indeed, The Right to Design integrates the rapidly increasing tendency of the Internet of Things and Smart Cities to show that, in reality, we must move toward the Internet of We. Over the past five years, I 'purposefully' explored the tangency between mindfulness and technology and looked for ways to bring these abstract ideas into reality. Through a series of interactive installations called Mindfulness Engineering in Action, I created a space for fundamental questions such to the direction of human relationships and the importance and health benefits of having dedicated moments of Mindfulness in all walks of our lives.

The collected data and the documented insights gained from these interactive installations[1] revealed to me that the next step of expansion of the theory of Mindfulness Engineering™ should focus on extending critical elements of mindfulness to the technological world. These installations also provoked deeper questions about the future of AI, and its nexus and interface with the field of human emotions, desires, dreams and needs, such as the need for intimacy, integrity, authenticity, and inclusion in the emerging digital

---

[1]   www.cos-collective.com/art-stream-shima-beigi/

age. The combination of these concepts and ideas has shaped the pillar of The Right to Design component of designing a Mindful and Smart City.

The Right to Becoming

The Right to Becoming is about becoming Mindfully Smart in the Globalised, Urbanised and Digitalised (GUD) World.

BUT HOW? By letting go of command-and-control models, by distributing power among citizens, and by embracing the unknown. While the Mindful Smart City Manifesto speaks about designing for people and embracing change, the desire for finding a practical recipe for the future of cities should not limit our imagination in its provision of competing future urban scenarios.

With the growing impact of climate change on urban systems, the rising demand for building socially inclusive urban systems, the rising awareness of the powerful role of technology in shaping both social fabric and urban architecture, and the rising evidence of patterns of change in the criteria for living – and therefore change in people's choices as to where to settle – we are witnessing a growing desire to label cities. We can additionally track this expansive pattern of labelling cities (i.e., happy cities, sustainable cities, green cities, playful cities, and so on), in an attempt to make sense of the highly complex and wicked matters of GUD.

I coined GUD to emphasise that humanity is moving towards increasingly organismic systems. This means that our systems are becoming more susceptible to having detrimental impacts upon each other. If we continue to expand mindlessly (i.e., without changing the paradigm of urban living, thinking and being), we cannot survive the complex challenges ahead, let alone thrive. In this transition, human development depends on 'collective acts of togetherness' in order to progress toward a more sustainable and inclusive collective state.

Additionally, it is necessary for Smart City stakeholders to observe and realise ways in which Mother Nature operates. Recent research on the resilience and sustainability of urban systems emphasises that treating humans and non-human entities as equal is a first step in overcoming the dichotomy between social and ecological. Equally, by treating social and technological as single integrated systems, we can shape the direction of technological systems. In short, we do not own Earth, and, equally, technology cannot overcome Earth. At best, it can co-evolve with natural systems.

In developing Mindfulness Engineering™, I noticed that the engineering community is dominated by an overwhelming desire to mechanically conceptualise and define the world. With this mechanical mindset, buildings and structures are neither dynamic nor fluid. In this fixed Western mindset, engineers and developers of technology do not think about the impacts of their designs on the wellbeing and consciousness of humans.

However, the system of life operates beyond the limited capacity of engineering and technological designs. In the language of Eastern traditions, life flows. In these ever-changing systems of life, fitness is not about building stronger systems that can survive change. Rather, those that can think differently and move with change, learn from it, and create more inclusive and knowledge-based communities, are the ones that survive, thrive and transcend.

The Right to Becoming and the Epigenetics of Mindful Smart Cities

The boundary between science and spirituality is no longer rigid. Thanks to the language of system thinking, different branches of science and spirituality have begun to merge. Epigenetics is one of these concepts that I want to speak about. The concept of epigenetics is essentially about how genes interact with the surrounding space. Once studied in depth, we realise that our systems are not designed to demonstrate such a degree of 'plasticity'.

In the development of the theory of Mindfulness Engineering™, I investigated social-ecological and socio-technical systems' resilience and adaptation strategies. I also elaborated upon how the process of resilience intricately resembles the processes of epigenetics. First, let's look at the underlying process of Epigenetics.

The concept of the 'Epigenetic Landscape' was introduced by evolutionary biologist Conrad Waddington. Epigenetic is a term defined as "the branch of biology which studies the causal interactions between genes and their products, which bring the phenotype into being" (Waddington, 1953). Epigenetics, in a broad sense, is a bridge between genotype and phenotype, a phenomenon that changes the final outcome of a locus or chromosome without changing the underlying DNA sequence. For example, even though the vast majority of cells within a multicellular organism share an identical genotype, organismal development generates a diversity of cell types with disparate, yet stable, profiles of gene expression and distinct cellular functions.

Specifically, epigenetics may be defined as the study of any potentially stable and, ideally, heritable change in gene expression or cellular phenotype that occurs without changes in Watson-Crick base-pairing of DNA. Thus, cellular differentiation may be considered an epigenetic phenomenon, largely governed by changes in the 'epigenetic landscape', as opposed to alterations in genetic inheritance. Covalent modification, nucleosome remodelling, and histone variants work together to introduce meaningful variation into the chromatin fibre, and their collective contribution to epigenetics is only now being rigorously explored. According to Golberg et al. (2007), it is becoming clear that significant cross-communication exists between different epigenetic pathways. These complex dynamics already control our bodies at the cellular and systemic levels. As complex adaptive individuals, we humans originate from different backgrounds. These historical differences, while making us unique at the individual level, can cause friction at the systemic level. For instance, being attached to one's own worldview hinders the flow of new information. Because humans are naturally adaptive, they can also learn to manage, modify and change their adaptability for either good or bad. As we grow up, we expand, and with this expansion comes change. Sometimes we lose touch with our core essence. In these circumstances, it's worthwhile to look toward ancient knowledge, because this often offers a counter-intuitive way back to our core essence. For example, In the Tao Te Ching, Lao Tzu poses the question "How do I know the way of all things at the Beginning? By what is within me". *Tao* or *Dao* literally means 'way', and implies the essential, unnameable process of the universe. *Teh* or *Te* means 'virtue' or 'integrity' and *Ching* or *Jing* in this context means 'great book' or 'classic'. We need to make adjustments in order to retain our core identity. This desire to preserve one's identity is a powerful resource for resilience at the individual level. In psychological resilience, for example, the resilience of individuals is highly linked to their desire to draw resources from the external environment in order to transform the negative impacts of shocks on their lives. My research on the resilience of complex systems and designing Smart Cities made me realise that building a collective and systemic level of resilience is achievable. However, the surrounding environmental and social systems need to be in synchronisation with one another. To illustrate this, we can think of the Epigenetic Landscape described earlier. Epigenetic describes the cell differentiation process as the path taken by a ball through branching valleys, each of which represents a developmental state. Figure 1, adapted from Furusawa and Kaneko (2012), helps visualise how cells undergo the process of differentiation. In this figure, Furusawa and Kaneko show that at the cellular level, stem cells can both robustly proliferate in the same valley and differentiate, i.e. switch valleys (Fig.1-B).

In a more elaborate model (Figure 2), Furusawa and Kaneko further demonstrate that as cells undergo the process of differentiation a complex chain of communications takes places. Communication, and positive and negative feedback loops, influence which gene is eventually expressed.

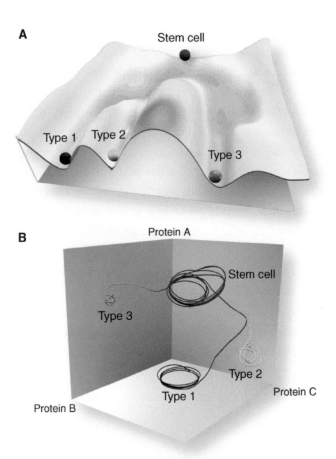

Figure 1. A. Waddington's Epigenetic Landscape. The development of a cellular state is represented by a ball rolling down a landscape of bifurcating valleys, each representing different cell types. **B. Dynamical-systems representation of cellular states.** Each axis represents the expression of a protein whose time development is depicted as a trajectory in space. Final states are attractors and correspond to distinct cell types. (Furusawa and Kaneko 2012)

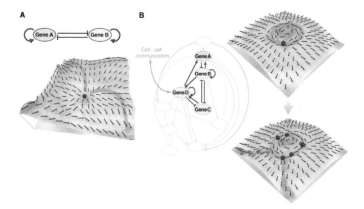

Figure 2. A. Dynamical-Systems view on the differentiation dynamics of a stem cell. By adding self-activation (top, red arrows) to a toggle-switch network, i.e., two mutually repressing genes (bottom), an attractor (red) with balanced expression of the two genes is added between A-activated and B-activated attractors (green and blue, respectively). Differentiation from the balanced expression to either of the biased attractors is triggered by noise. **B. Oscillatory gene expression dynamics** (upper right: circulating trajectory shown by an orange arrow) are generated by negative feedback in the regulation network (left, red and black arrows). Cell differentiation is driven by cell-cell communication (green arrow) and fixed through positive feedback in the network An increase in cell numbers results in some cells leaving the original attractor (stem cell state) to differentiate, whereas those that remain proliferate (lower: orange trajectory bifurcates owing to cell-cell interactions). Orange and blue arrows on the landscape represent the trajectory of cellular state and the gradient of the landscape that affect the movement of the ball, respectively. (Furusawa and Kaneko 2012)

These complex dynamics already exist in our bodies at the cellular level. By explicitly bringing them to an immediate collective awareness, and connecting the concept of epigenetic to the relationship between society and technology, my aim is to offer novel ways in which to reimagine this critical nexus. Technical and technological systems influence collective behaviour.

The Right to Design Is Directly Connected to the Right to Becoming

I argue that experts' mindsets and awareness of technology, design, and architecture of technical systems influence the moods of people and direct their behaviour. A Smart City is a continuation of such a way of thinking and level of awareness. If it is designed from a capitalist point of view, i.e. prioritising utility over people, the city becomes a mechanically enabled machine with a limited capacity for being truly relatable from the perspective of the human experience. This city is about connected objects – IoT – rather than connected people – IoP.

A Mindful Smart City is different, because it is built from a vantage point and consciousness of a WE SPACE. This WE SPACE is filled with pockets of awareness of the collective Rights of Citizens. This means, similar to manifestation of genes under the impact of the epigenetic landscape, our future smart cities will demonstrate what we practice, our level consciousness, awareness and mindfulness can dramatically push the envelope of design toward Mindful Smart Cities, cities that are about humans and not objects. Mindful Smart Cities promote the internet of people and not merely of objects and things.

In Mindful Smart Cities, everybody becomes aware that connected objects or things create this pervasive illusion of connectivity. Contrary to this illusion of connection through things and objects, heartfully and emotionally connected people create a field of consciousness filled with hope, love, empathy, happiness, belonging, compassion and inclusivity.

A Set of Introspective Questions for Future Generations of Researchers, Designers, Urban Theorists, Artists and People

- Can we embed such insights into our cities so that they support our mind-body evolution?
- Is it possible that, at the social and technical level, the complex network of interconnected technical systems influences behavioural patterns of social agents in a similar way to which environmental factors such as quality and type of nutrients and parental care influence biological systems?

CHAPTER 6

THE RIGHT TO TECHNOLOGY

What Does the Right to Technology Mean?

The Right to Technology means realising that technology connects. But it is the human spirit that transforms our technological platforms into an inclusive space of collective expansion. I consider this space a 'WE SPACE'. This WE SPACE is about reframing the way we see the world. By incorporating Eastern and Western philosophies of change into Mindfulness Engineering™ I attempt to develop the capacity of social agents for speaking in a shared language that is appropriate for the emergence of a Mindful Smart City. To develop such an ability, Mindfulness Engineering™ invites the designer to consider social agents akin to the flow of energy; movement and stillness at the same time, in a continuous state of flux.

If becoming better at managing change is our goal, then we must learn how to move toward engineering more health-generating living spaces. To attempt to enhance the inner mental landscape of social agents to not only do the thinking, but also to become adept at speaking and acting. This requires us to dig deeper into the realm of emotions (i.e., energy motions). In short, the Right to Technology is about going beyond pleasure principles as the driving force of human behaviour. The Right to Technology is about bringing awareness and consciousness into the digital world. Increasing access to ICT must be in line with societal readiness for adopting ICT platforms and their ability to make sense of data and contribute to the process of knowledge and wisdom creation.

Where Is the 'I' in 'Ai'?

Before the emergence of digitalisation, the relationship between mind and action used to be discussed with a reference to the work of French philosopher Descartes. Before digitalisation, thinking the experience of one's existence was directly connected to thinking (i.e. I *think therefore I am*). But, today, thanks to mass digitalisation, our internal world, and therefore our sense of self, is radically changing. We are geared up with technological gadgets and devices. These objects not only change us, but also our relationships. At the level of collectives, we need to rethink the current disconnect between technology and humanity of our relationships. We should search for the realness of the 'I' in AI. This is particularly important in shaping the future of smart cities and smart citizenship.

Psycho-Cybernetics, Selfies and Information Addiction

Maltz was amazed by the dramatic impact of plastic surgery on people's self-image. He noticed that when people change their facial features their personality changes as well. So he argued there is a non-physical facet to human personality. This non-physical and invisible side is highly influenced by how people perceive themselves. For example, if they think they are scattered, distorted, ugly, inferior, they will behave accordingly. In other words, people's outward expression becomes a function of their internal ecology. In Maltz's view, this dynamic was a classic cybernetic problem, hence calling his method of healing Psycho-Cybernetic. Norbet Wiener defines cybernetics as the study of regulatory processes in both living and nonliving systems. By taking into account the underlying concepts of cybernetics aka feedback loops, Maltz concluded that if by improving the visual features the non-physical facet of humans helps smoothing their behaviour, then maybe the root of discord is in the self-image. Therefore, by removing dysfunctional belief systems, emotional scars, individuals self-heal and self-correct without even doing any plastic surgery (Maltz, 1960). The self-image is a construction of one's imagination. Thus, it also carries hidden information about one's subconscious mind.

The subconscious mind in its very essence, creates the 'area of possible' for the individual. This area of possibility secretly contributes to one's success and failure in facing life's challenges. Now, with this critical information in mind, I propose a set of questions:

A Set of Introspective Questions for Future Generations of Researchers, Designers, Urban Theorists, Artists and People
- Are we moving toward too great a level of individualism at the expense of inclusivity?
- How can we address the complex trade-offs of sustainability between society, environment, economy and governance within the Smart City Agenda?

What Does the Right to Information Mean, and Why Does It Matter?

As people start to engage with the flow of information by means of smart devices, a richer dimension of human life begins to permeate and extend into the collective field of information. The boundaries between the real and the virtual are no longer rigid. Information is becoming richer and richer. But what about our lives? How can we strike a balance between diverse streams of intelligence? Data-driven does not equal data-enabled. The Right to Information means Making Room for the Mindful in the Search for Smartness.

The Yin and Yang of the Field(s) of Information

The relationship(s) between technology, societal readiness for technological adoption and human needs is not mechanical. It is complex, nonlinear, and organic. Mindfully connected citizens are the engine of urban change in the city of the future (Beigi, 2019).

A smart city isn't created by people simply responding to inputs, but by citizens performing an essential role: the leading role in the process of data collection and sharing (Ratti, 2012). Socio-technological literacy has to be the new language (Turkle, 2012), and this doesn't merely imply learning to code. We can only unlock the vast potential of AI and the technological industry for human progress if we discuss both the bright and the not-so-bright sides.

We can only design 'for' and 'with' humans if we investigate ways in which technology affects our human relationships, social norms and behaviours. The Mindful Smart City acts as an invitation to move toward an *actography of uncertainty in our complex system*. Mindfulness Engineering places a focus on the creation of WE SPACES (Beigi, 2019). This dynamic, ever-changing ecosystem presented in the 21st century means that we are more likely to need a road map to navigate from the Known Knowns, into Known Unknowns, Unknown Unknowns, and Unknown Knowns.

The solution to this transition is working together as a conscious global community. For this level of collaboration to emerge, we must nevertheless undergo not only a deep mental model transformation, but also a deep scientific revolution. We can solve the grand challenges of our times only by connecting ideas from different disciplines. And this means, undergoing a fundamental transformation of ourselves (mentally, physically, scientifically and spiritually).

Moving beyond the Pleasure Principle

In investigating the elusive concept of 'Smartness', we must pose a set of questions regarding what 'smart' actually is. The concept of Smartness somehow connects all stakeholders because of the underlying theme of our interests, i.e. attaining a higher quality of urban wellbeing. During this research, I noticed that the common ground of sustainable information can guide urban digitalisation towards finding unity in this diverse landscape of GUD.

To make room for the mindful in smart, an emphasis should be placed on methods which direct information flows toward sustainability and knowledge. In this regard, technological companies are responsible for attempting to shift communities towards mindful interactions with data rather than promoting addictive patterns.

The key message here is that citizens have a right to design, technology, and information. It is therefore necessary to develop legal systems that push the digital landscape in the direction of dignified knowledge.

Why should one accomplish more every day? Are we in some form of competition? Even so, if I want to accomplish more, research suggests that I am actually better off 'turning my smartphone off' and focusing on the present moment without constant background noise. The profit-oriented and short-sighted nature of current technological industries misinforms people about the power of technology, distracts them from depending on their critical skills such as agency, self-mastery, focus, creativity and discipline. In short, I think we are moving too far and too fast in overestimating technology's power while underestimating human capacity. This technological bubble is an illusion. It needs a reality check.

CHAPTER 7

PRESERVING THE RIGHT TO BECOMING IN THE AGE OF GUD

In *The Age of Surveillance Capitalism*, Zuboff (2019) sets out a case for freedom of expression in the digital age. Big tech companies have made fortunes from people's data. In many marketing cases, this data is mined without any form of consent. This overwhelmingly asymmetric power structure is maintained through sophisticated psychological strategies.

People simply do not know how their data is being used, when it is extracted, by whom, or for what kind(s) of purpose(s). Even worse, they do not have any awareness of the inner workings of the Tech Industry Black Box. The more these players at the top of the hierarchy gain power over people and their data, the more our collective right to freedom of expression and democracy is undermined. When we think of the consequences of such an ill-structured power dynamic between people and the tech industry, it is evident that our collective human experience is at stake.

In the language of Zuboff: "...Right now we are at the beginning of a new era that I have called information civilization, and it repeats the same dangerous arrogance. The aim is not to dominate nature but rather human nature. The focus has shifted from machines that overcome the limits of bodies to machines that modify the behaviour of individuals, groups, and populations in the service of market objectives. This global installation of instrumentation power overcomes and replaces the human inwardness that feeds the will and gives sustenance to our voices in the first person" (Zuboff, 2019).

Democracy and freedom of expression are two concepts that will always have to be subjected to the test of time. And, sometimes, in the so-called age of interconnectedness, they need us to fight back stronger. Technology and ICT platforms have already penetrated every aspect of the urban experience. In other words, the so-called Smart City is already here!

But, can we steer the direction of this pervasive technological urban experience toward democracy, freedom of expression and citizen participation without fighting for our legitimate Right to The City?

To preserve the Right to City, or better to mention the Right to the Smart City, the Mindful Smart City is defined as a WE SPACE. A WE SPACE is a space where we share our humanity as opposed to our data. Data is a by-product of our current technological capabilities. Therefore, it is not reflective of our humanity and our being. I coined The Right to Becoming in this Manifesto to show that, when designing a Mindful Smart City, we must think in terms of a WE SPACE, be mindful of the direction of technological development, and participate in the protection of our humanity. In brief, the Right to Becoming means Mindfulness can be extended into technological platforms and manifest itself as SMARTFULNESS®.

Why Should Smart Cities Care about the Right to Becoming?

The importance of The Right to Becoming can be further seen in the future of the urban economy, and in particular under the umbrella of the Sharing Economy. The Sharing Economy is an ICT-enabled economic system whereby individuals can move beyond being passive consumers of goods, services and products. The Sharing Economy has transformed not only traditional businesses, but also the traditional definition of work or labour. Today, millions of people are leaving their jobs to find and start their own businesses, for both sociological and psychological reasons. This practice of following a different value system is projected to significantly rise in the future (Makimoto and Manners, 1997; Malone and Laubacher, 1998). In short, people want to leave the comfort of their jobs, and move beyond the Rat Race, to become what are termed 'Digital Nomads'. Digital nomads are defined as a community of workers situated at the confluence of four elements: sense of self, digital community, creativity and eccentricity, and mobility.

The nomadicity movement is having a powerful impact on propagation of memes, aka the unit of transmitting socio-cultural codes (Blackmore, 2000) across the digital landscape. As nomads move from one location to another, they will be exposed to complex information. Many of these individuals are also in danger of loneliness and social isolation. To compensate for this, they build their own communities which in return lead to emergence of new individual codes of behaviours and belief systems.

These isolated views in the vicinity of other digital nomads form 'new collective cognitive models' which might not be sustainable and practical for the whole of humanity. Our ability to create cohesion and resilience in this emerging data-driven and data-enabled future is highly dependent on our capacity to verify the large stream of data that percolates into our awareness. Digital Nomadicity is an early sign of people rising up to fulfil their own power. While this shift threatens many industries, this shift of human potential is positive, because it can force the labour market to transform. Once people leave their comfort zones, they move towards liberation of their potentials and self-actualisation. These transformed individuals will then become the new founding pillars of a real democracy.

That is why, through the lens of Mindfulness Engineering™, I consider protecting the Right to Becoming of urban dwellers to be fundamentally interdependent with the way technology translates and augments into future smart cities. In this Manifesto, I call for a fundamental educational plan on the nature of data and information, development of a new code of ethics and behaviour (e.g., a verification system) within cyberspace, recalling humanity's Right to Becoming. For this to happen, I suggest the integration of elements of mindfulness into smart city design and a shift in the evolution of technology towards consciousness and awareness of a bigger picture. SMARTFULNESS *is* this bigger picture: technology in the service of human expansion, and a cooperative ally of the Right to Becoming.

Smartfulness® Means Holding Space for Others

In my quest to discover more about how the future of work can be envisioned, to investigate the role that technology plays in shaping the structure of governance systems, and to find out how a space for Mindfulness can be created, I spent three months living and working as a digital nomad in Bali. Bali is a highly sought after destination for 'nomadicity'; its breath-taking landscape, combined with an undercurrent of potent spiritual energy, makes it an excellent place to observe how digitalisation responds to these pre-existing forces. Abound in esoteric-based hubs, I discovered one specific location that attracts a large proportion of digital nomads resident in Ubud; Sayuri Healing Food, founded by Sayuri Tanaka, a Japanese raw food Chef. At Sayuri, you can find an international community of people who have somehow discovered that the 'business as usual' mentality, the silo mentality, is no longer viable. To find a new trajectory of expansion, these explorers have left their classic jobs, headed to Bali, and are busy creating their new state of being. The Spirit of the Sayuri Healing Cafe is rooted in the Japanese philosophy of life. At its core, the cafe embraces cycles of life and change. What 'smart' means here is entirely different to the scientific notion of smart. Here, smart means holding a space for each other, embracing a new culture of food and plant-based medicine, and finding ways to connect to something bigger than the individual.

Smartfulness® Means Connection to a Higher Consciousness, and Having a Perception of a Higher Level of Smartness

During the final phase of writing this Manifesto, I travelled to India to find out what 'smart' could possibly mean for a country on the rise. And, I could not find any city better than Varanasi to describe the essence of urban life and finalise this Manifesto.

The holy city of Varanasi, is one of the oldest cities in the world. Varanasi (or Benares) is set on the banks of the Ganges River, in Uttar Pradesh. With its proximity to Sarnath, the place where Buddha preached his first sermon after enlightenment, the city has transformed to a symbol of devotion to gods, culture, spirituality and learning. Varanasi defies all the rules, standards and regulations that one might imagine. Perhaps, these lines by Mark Twain best describe it: "... Benares is older than history, older than tradition, older even than legend, and looks twice as old as all of them put together."

Here, smart means being temporally aligned with the currents of Mother Ganges; a belief exists that the Ganges has its origins in the trees of Lord Shiva and in Varanasi. Smart means letting fully go. Smart means seeing the death, seeing the joy, seeing the primordiality of life and walking away with total silence. Smart means not asking logical questions. Smart means finding life's full circle. Smart means moving beyond common sense. Smart means paying intense attention to colours, smells and tastes. Smart means letting go of your own notion of common sense and allowing a greater pull to move you.

Technology is only a mechanical instrument that creates better connections between objects. Technology is mechanical. Artificial intelligence is artificial.

The cores of Consciousness, faith, empathy, desire to be a part of something bigger than yourself and love are rooted in the sole real technology: HUMAN HEART.

WHAT IS NEXT?

Our ability to create cohesion and resilience in this emerging data-driven and data-enabled future is highly dependent on our capacity to verify the large stream of data that percolates into our awareness. Hence, there is a pressing need for a fundamental educational plan on the nature of data and information, and development of new code of ethics and behaviour (for instance, a verification system) in cyberspace. In other words, we can integrate elements of mindfulness into smart city design, and move toward smartfulness, soulfulness and mindfulness. The Mindful Smart City Manifesto is the first technology-related Manifesto written by a female scientist. I hope that this work will pave the way for future generations of female leaders in the field. Further, the Mindful Smart City Manifesto is the first body of research that extends citizens' Right to the City to The Right to Technology, The Right to Information, The Right to Design, and The Right to Becoming. Today, we are at a critical socio-technical, socio-cultural and environmental tipping point. We must wake up and realise that what connects humanity is not merely technology or the application of sophisticated machines. Humans are connected through real and authentic relationships.

Technology Connects. But, it is the human connection that brings consciousness.

REFERENCES

Anthopoulos, L., Fitsilis, P., 2013. Using Classification and Roadmapping techniques for Smart City viability's realization. *Electronic Journal of e-Government 11*.

Bakıcı, T., Almirall, E., and Wareham, J., 2012. A Smart City Initiative: The Case of Barcelona, *Journal of the Knowledge Economy 2*: 1, 1–14.

Barrionuevo, J.M., Berrone, P., Ricart, J.E., 2012. Smart cities, sustainable progress. *IESE Insight 14*, 50–57.

Beigi S. A Road Map for Cross Operationalization of Resilience. In *The Science of Hormesis in Health and Longevity 2019 Jan 1* (pp. 235-242). Academic Press.

Beigi, S., 2015. Mindfulness Engineering™: a theory of resilience for the volatile, uncertain, complex and ambiguous (VUCA) world. University of Bristol.

Blackmore S, Blackmore SJ. The meme machine. Oxford Paperbacks; 2000 Mar 16.

Caragliu, A., Del Bo, C., Nijkamp, P., 2009. Smart cities in Europe. Research Memoranda Series 0048 (VU University Amsterdam, Faculty of Economics, Business Administration and Econometrics). CRC Press, Boca Raton.

Caragliu, A., Del Bo, C., Nijkamp, P., 2011. Smart cities in Europe. *Journal of urban technology 18*, 65–82.

Castells M. Informationalism, networks, and the network society: a theoretical blueprint. The network society: A cross-cultural perspective. 2004:3-45.

Castells, M., 2009. Rise of the Network Society, With a New Preface: The Information Age: Economy, Society, and Culture Volume I.

Chen, T., 2010. Smart grids, smart cities need better networks [Editor's Note]. *IEEE Network 24*, 2–3.

Coletta, C., Kitchin, R., 2017. Algorithmic governance: Regulating the "heartbeat" of a city using the Internet of Things. Big Data & Society 4, 205395171774241–. https://doi.org/10.1177/2053951717742418

Cretu, G.L., 2012. Smart Cities Design Using Event-driven Paradigm and Semantic Web, *Informatica Economica 16*: 4 (2012) 57–67.

Desdemoustier, J., Crutzen, N., 2015. Smart Cities en Belgique : Analyse qualitative de 11 projets. University of Liege, Liege.

Eger, J.M., 2009. Smart growth, smart cities, and the crisis at the pump a worldwide phenomenon. I-WAYS-*The Journal of E-Government Policy and Regulation 32*, 47–53.

Fathy, T.A., 1991. Telecity: information technology and its impact on city form. Greenwood Publishing Group Inc.

Ferrell, J.E., Bistability, Bifurcations, and Waddington's Epigenetic Landscape. *Current Biology, 2012. 22*(11): p. R458-R466.

Furusawa, C. and K. Kaneko, A dynamical-systems view of stem cell biology. *Science, 2012. 338*(6104): p. 215-217.

Gardner, H.E., 2000. Intelligence reframed: Multiple intelligences for the 21st century. Hachette UK.

Guan, L., 2012. Smart Steps To A Battery City, *Government News 32*: 2, 24–27.

Giffinger, R., Fertner, C., Kramar, H., Kalasek, R., Pichler-Milanović, N., Meijers, E., 2007. Smart cities: Ranking of european medium-sized cities. Vienna, austria: Centre of regional science (srf), Vienna university of technology. www. smart-cities. eu/download/smart cities final report. pdf.

Giffinger, R., Gudrun, H., 2010. Smart cities ranking: an effective instrument for the positioning of the cities? *ACE: Architecture, City and Environment 4*, 7–26.

Greenfield, A., 2013. Against the Smart City: A Pamphlet. This is Part I of" The City is Here to Use. Do projects.

Hall, R.E., Bowerman, B., Braverman, J., Taylor, J., Todosow, H., Von Wimmersperg, U., 2000. The vision of a Smart City. Brookhaven National Lab., Upton, NY (US).

Harrison, C., Eckman, B. Hamilton, R., Hartswick, P., Kalagnanam, J., Paraszczak, J., and Williams, P., 2010. Foundations for Smarter Cities, *IBM Journal of Research and Development 54*: 4, 1–16.

Harvey, D., 2008. The right to the city. The City Reader 6, 23–40.

Hollands, R.G., 2008. Will the real Smart City please stand up? Intelligent, progressive or entrepreneurial? *City 12*, 303–320.

Institute of Mechanical Engineers, 2013. NATURAL DISASTERS SAVING LIVES TODAY, BUILDING RESILIENCE FOR TOMORROW.

Ishida, T., Isbister, K., 2000. Digital cities: technologies, experiences, and future perspectives. Springer Science & Business Media.

Isin, E.F., 2002. City, democracy and citizenship: Historical images, contemporary practices. Handbook of citizenship studies, 305–316.

Jacobs, J., 1964. The death and life of great American cities. Wiley Online Library.

Kelly, K., 2010. What technology wants. Penguin.

Komninos, N., 2011. Intelligent cities: Variable geometries of spatial intelligence. *Intelligent Buildings International 3*, 172–188.

Komninos, N., Sefertzi, E., n.d. Intelligent Cities.

Kourtit, K. and Nijkamp, P., 2012. Smart Cities in the Innovation Age, *Innovation: The European Journal of Social Science Research 25*: 2, 93–95.

Kourtit, K., Nijkamp, P. and Arribas, D., 2012. Smart Cities in Perspective – A Comparative European Study by Means of Self-organizing Maps, *Innovation: The European Journal of Social Science Research 25*: 2, 229–246.

Krivý, M., 2016. Towards a critique of cybernetic urbanism: The Smart City and the society of control. Planning Theory 1473095216645631.

Lazaroiu, G.C. and Roscia, M., 2012. Definition Methodology for the Smart Cities Model, *Energy 47*: 1, 326 – 332.

Lazaroiu, G.C., Roscia, M., 2012. Definition methodology for the smart cities model. *Energy 47*, 326–332.

Lee, J.H., Hancock, M.G., Hu, M.-C., 2014. Towards an effective framework for building smart cities: Lessons from Seoul and San Francisco. *Technological Forecasting and Social Change 89*, 80–99.

Lefebvre, H., 1996. The right to the city. Writings on cities 63181.

Lefebvre, H., The Urban Revolution, Minneapolis 2003; and Writings on Cities, Oxford 1996.

Legg, S., Hutter, M., 2006. A formal measure of machine intelligence. arXiv preprint cs/0605024.

Legg, S., Hutter, M., 2007. Universal intelligence: A definition of machine intelligence. *Minds and Machines 17*, 391– 444.

Lombardi, P., Giordano, S., Farouh, H. and Yousef, W., 2012. Modelling the Smart City Performance, *Innovation: The European Journal of Social Science Research 25*: 2, 137–149.

Makimoto, T., and Manners, D. 1997. Digital Nomad. Wiley.

Malone, T. W., and Laubacher, R. J. 1998. The Dawn of the E-Lance Economy, *Harvard Business Review* (76:5), p. 144.

Manville, C., 2014. Mapping Smart City in the EU. European Parliament. Retrieved February 5, 2014.

Marsal-Llacuna, M.L., Colomer-Llinàs, J. and Meléndez-Frigola, J., 2014. Lessons in urban monitoring taken from sustainable and livable cities to better address the Smart Cities initiative, Technological Fore-casting and Social Change.

Mino, E., 1999. Experiences of European digital cities, in: Digital Cities. Springer, pp. 58–72.

Mitchell, W.J., 1999. Designing the digital city, in: Digital Cities. Springer, pp. 1–6.

Next Generation Internet - An Open Internet Initiative [WWW Document], 2017. URL http://ec.europa.eu/research/participants/portal/desktop/en/opportunities/h2020/topics/ict-24-2018-2019.html (accessed 12.26.17).

Nam, T. and Pardo, T.A. Conceptualizing Smart City with Dimensions of Technology, People, and Institutions," Proc. 12th Conference on Digital Government Research, College Park, MD, June 12– 15, 2011.

Nash, C., Jarrahi, M.H., Sutherland, W., Phillips, G., 2018. Digital nomads beyond the buzzword: Defining digital nomadic work and use of digital technologies, in: International Conference on Information. Springer, pp. 207–217.

Purcell, M., 2014. Possible worlds: Henri Lefebvre and the right to the city. *Journal of Urban Affairs 36*, 141–154.

Ratti, C., 2013. Smart City, smart citizen. EGEA spa.

Rodrigues, N., 2016. Algorithmic Governmentality, Smart Cities and Spatial Justice. justice spatiale-spatial justice 10, http–www.

Sadowski, J., Pasquale, F.A., 2015. The spectrum of control: A social theory of the Smart City.

Shanahan, M., 2012. Satori before singularity. *Journal of Consciousness Studies 19*, 87–102.

Shanahan, M., 2015. The technological singularity. MIT Press.

Thite, M., 2011. Smart Cities: Implications of Urban Planning for Human Resource Development, *Human Resource Development International* 14: 5, 623–631.

Thuzar, M., 2011. Urbanization in SouthEast Asia: Developing Smart Cities for the Future?," *Regional Outlook*, 96–100.

Van Bastelaer, B., 1998. Digital Cities and transferability of results, in: 4th EDC Conference on Digital Cities, Salzburg. pp. 61–70.

Van den Besselaer, P., Melis, I., Beckers, D., 1999. Digital cities: organization, content, and use, in: Digital Cities. Springer, pp. 18–32.

Waddington, C.H., Epigenetic and Evolution. Symposia of the Society for Experimental Biology, 1953. 7: p. 186-199.

Washburn, D., Sindhu, U., Balaouras, S., Dines, R.A., Hayes, N., Nelson, L.E., 2009. Helping CIOs understand "Smart City" initiatives. *Growth* 17, 1–17.

Wu, W., 2005. Dynamic cities and creative clusters. World Bank Publications.

Zuboff S. The age of surveillance capitalism: The fight for a human future at the new frontier of power. Profile Books; 2019 Jan 31.

Zygiaris, S., 2013. Smart City Reference Model: Assisting Planners to Conceptualize the Building of Smart City Innovation Ecosystems, *Journal of the Knowledge Economy* 4: 2, 217–231.